HONEY

Fireflies, Honey, and Silk

GILBERT WALDBAUER

WITH ILLUSTRATIONS BY JAMES NARDI

University of California Press *Berkeley Los Angeles London*

The publisher gratefully acknowledges the generous support of the General Endowment Fund of the University of California Press Foundation.

University of California Press, one of the most distinguished university presses in the United States, enriches lives around the world by advancing scholarship in the humanities, social sciences, and natural sciences. Its activities are supported by the UC Press Foundation and by philanthropic contributions from individuals and institutions. For more information, visit www.ucpress.edu.

University of California Press
Berkeley and Los Angeles, California

University of California Press, Ltd.
London, England

Library of Congress Cataloging-in-Publication Data
Waldbauer, Gilbert.
Fireflies, honey, and silk / Gilbert Waldbauer. With illustrations by James Nardi.
p. cm.
Includes bibliographical references and index.
ISBN 978-0-520-25883-9 (cloth : alk. paper)
1. Beneficial insects. I. Title.
SF517.W35 2009 2008047713
595.7'163—dc22

Manufactured in the United States of America
18 17 16 15 14 13 12 11 10 09
10 9 8 7 6 5 4 3 2 1
The paper used in this publication meets the minimum requirements of ANSI/NISO Z39.48–1992 (R 1997) (*Permanence of Paper*).

To John Henry Comstock of Cornell University,
the father of academic entomology,
and to his wife, Anna Botsford Comstock,
who pioneered the teaching of nature study at Cornell

Contents

Illustrations

Note

As you read this book, you will come across quotations from or references to the work of scientists and other writers. It is only fair that you have the opportunity to read and evaluate these publications on your own. In the Selected References section at the back of the book, you will find bibliographic citations, listed by author, that will lead you to these published sources for each chapter. People who provided me with unpublished information are identified in the text but are not listed in the Selected References.

Introduction

My fascination with insects began on a sunny winter day during grade school in Bridgeport, Connecticut, when I found a big brown cocoon on an apple tree. I had heard that some insects survive the winter snugly encased in silken cocoons, but I wasn't certain that this thing was a cocoon and hadn't the vaguest idea of what kind of insect might emerge from it in the spring. Nevertheless, I took it home and put it in a glass jar with a metal top pierced with air holes. Weeks later, the most beautiful and amazing insect I had ever seen emerged from it. Its broad wings spanned at least 5 inches and were gorgeously patterned with red, white, black, and a little violet. The antennae were big and featherlike. (I later learned that this is characteristic of males of many moths.) I thought it was a butterfly, but my teacher told me that it was a cecropia moth and that butterflies don't spin cocoons. (Now I know that a few actually do.) From that moment on I was hooked on natural history, especially insects. I began a collection and identified grasshoppers, beetles, butterflies, and other insects with Frank Lutz's splendid *Field Book of Insects,* first published in 1918 but still useful today.

In June 1946, my graduating class at Central High School in Bridgeport held a banquet, followed by the reading of the class "will," which was actually a prophecy of what the future would hold for us. The will proclaimed, "Gilbert Waldbauer, professor of entomology at Yale University, leaves one well-mounted tarantula to anyone who will have it." I chuckled because I thought the prophecy impossible, but I did in fact become a professor of entomology (though without a mounted tarantula). Many years later, I once again focused my attention on the cecropia moth, the insect that had sparked my life-long career. My colleague and friend Jim Sternburg and I, with the help of several graduate students, spent several years doing laboratory and field research on the physiology and behavior of this marvelously interesting insect.

Most people are seldom aware of the many insects around them. They do take notice of mosquitoes, house flies, cockroaches, and other annoying insects. But to their own detriment, and to the detriment of humanity's collective ecological conscience, they unthinkingly assume that all other insects are boring or, even worse, repulsive and pestiferous. In 1946, when DDT—the first of the "miracle" insecticides—appeared on the market, I heard that a few ecological illiterates (fortunately a *very* few) rejoiced because they thought that we could now exterminate *all* of the insects and other creepy-crawlies. Like most people, they had no idea that insects as a group are essential to the survival of life on Earth as we know it and almost certainly to our own survival. Insects play many vital roles in nearly all terrestrial and freshwater ecosystems. Among other services, they pollinate most flowering plants other than grasses; disperse the seeds of many plants; provide food for birds, fish, and other animals; and help to return dung and dead animals and plants to the soil.

But this book is not about pestiferous insects or the ecological importance of insects. It is about the pleasure a few of them—butterflies, singing crickets, fireflies, and ladybird beetles—give many of us, and about the direct effect others have on our material culture. These insects not only have enhanced the lives of people in many different societies but also are absorbingly interesting themselves. A few of them are well known—at least by name—but many other insects that contribute to our material culture are little known.

Most people have heard that silk, that marvelously luxurious fabric, is woven from threads unraveled from the cocoons of the silkworm, but few know how silkworms—which are actually caterpillars—are raised or when, how, and by whom the value of their cocoons was discovered. We put honey on our pancakes and in our hot rum toddies, but most of us know little about the bees that produce the honey. Some have heard that honey bees have a dance language, but how many also know that the language has a "grammar," that it conveys information with admirable precision, and that biologists have deciphered it?

Other insects that have also contributed to our material culture are unsung heroes. Until synthetic dyes appeared in the nineteenth century, by far the best and most widely used red dye was derived from the bodies of tiny cactus-feeding insects. The main ingredient in shellac is a product of the Asian lac insect, and combining lac with beeswax makes sealing wax. Do you know that the best black inks are made from galls, tumorlike growths on oak trees caused by tiny wasps? The Chinese may well have learned to make paper by watching paper-making hornets and other wasps. The biblical manna from heaven was probably the sugary excrement of a sap-sucking aphid from which the Kurds of Iraq and Turkey still make a delicious candy. Do you know that certain maggots are used to clean severely infected wounds, and that their use is increasing as more bacteria become resistant to antibiotics?

Throughout history insects have been the subject of fanciful legends. In the first century of the common era, Gaius Plinius Secundus, the Roman encyclopedist also known as Pliny the Elder, confidently assured his readers that ants as big as wolves live and mine gold in the mountains north of India. It was said in England that the tiny deathwatch beetle (*Testobium rufovillosum*) can predict a death in a household. These beetles, which burrow in dead wood—lumber—may be very numerous in old buildings. Adult females signal to males by tapping their heads against the side of their tunnels, making a ticking sound that is audible to people. As Frank Cowan put it, "The clicking of a Death-watch is an omen of the death of someone in the house wherein it is heard." There are many other myths about insects, some even more fantastic than Pliny's tale and the deathwatch beetle's supposed ability to predict the future. You will find as you read on, however, that the true stories of insects and their benefits to us are even more interesting and marvelous than the myths about them.

I Insects People Like

Certain insects have long been favorites of people around the world. Let's examine a few of them, and also glance at a few others that humans have only grudgingly come to appreciate or admire.

Most people like or at least tolerate ladybird beetles. These charming little insects and their larvae are well known as devourers of aphids, and are among the most beneficial of the insects. But, generally speaking, people do not like ladybirds just because they help us defeat pest insects. (An exception is some gardeners who even buy semidormant ladybirds by the quart—at considerable expense—and release them in their gardens hoping to control aphids. But it is a futile effort. Soon after being released and waking up, the ladybirds fly off, dispersing far and wide to eat aphids elsewhere.)

People who would slap away any other insect that alights on their bodies welcome ladybirds, letting them crawl onto their hands and up their arms. But why? Friends and acquaintances—of both sexes—have told me that they don't mind ladybirds because they're cute. And so they are: chubby, nonthreatening little creatures, hemispherical in shape, and usually bright red and marked with large, round, black spots. Years ago, and perhaps even

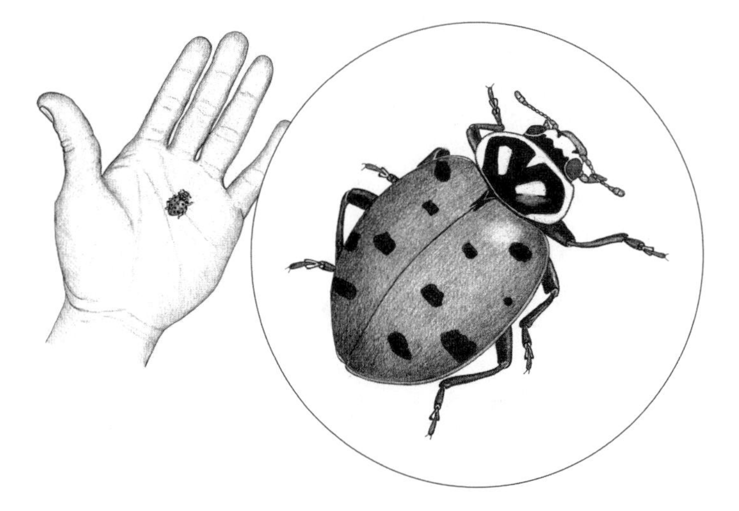

today, children who let a ladybird crawl on their hands would recite a nursery rhyme: "Ladybug, ladybug, fly away home,/Your house is on fire,/Your children will burn!"

Some languages, probably many more than I know of, have endearing names for ladybird beetles, names often derived from religious terms. Our English name is an abbreviated form of Our Lady's bird. Medieval European farmers, writes F. Tom Turpin, were well aware that aphids could and often did destroy their crops. Seeking to free their fields of these pests, they prayed to the Virgin Mary for help. Probably as often as not, ladybirds arrived, ate the aphids, saved the crop, and, consequently, were honored with the name Our Lady's beetle or Our Lady's bird. The Germans use a similar name, *Marienkäfer,* Mary's beetle. In Dutch, the ladybird is known as *Lieve-*

Above: A ladybird beetle crawls on the hand of a child who chants, "Ladybug, ladybug, fly away home."

heersbeestje, the dear Lord's little creature, and its French name is similar, *bête à bon Dieu,* the creature of God. In Greek ladybirds are called *paschalitsa,* the little ones of Easter, and an Israeli friend told me that in Hebrew they are known as *parat Moshe Rabbenu,* the creature of Rabbi Moses.

There is an exception to this love affair with ladybirds. When the multicolored Asian lady beetle (its "official" common name) invades our homes—as it often does—some consider it a pest. This stranger from the Orient was released in the United Sates to control other pest insects, but it did not become firmly established here until after it was introduced in 1988 to control aphids on pecan trees. It soon spread widely, but is most abundant in southern Canada and the northeastern states. The Asian lady beetle is not fond of us or our homes, but it finds a sheltered place to hibernate in winter by crawling into narrow openings in buildings in lieu of the crevices in the rocks of its homeland. Most become dormant and stay out of sight between the inner and outer walls, but a few blunder into a death trap, the living area, where, if not squashed by a finicky person, they are soon fatally desiccated by the winter dryness of the heated building.

The introduction of the aphid-eating Asian lady beetle is an example of biological control, defined as the use of one organism, such as an insect predator, parasite, or bacterium, to control a pest organism, usually an insect or a plant. The first and most successful application of biological control in the United States was the introduction of a ladybird beetle, the vedalia, to control the cottony cushion scale, a tiny sap-sucking scale insect—a relative of the aphids—that covers its body and egg mass with white, waxy threads. In 1886, this pest was spreading like wildfire through the citrus orchards of southern California, and was well on its way to obliterating the state's developing citrus industry. At that time there was no insecticide that would control these insects. It looked as if the citrus industry was doomed.

But Charles Valentine Riley, probably the greatest entomologist of that time, had a brilliant idea. He knew that the cottony cushion scale had been unintentionally brought to California from Australia, where it was uncommon and never destructive. He wondered why it was so destructive in California, where it was so abundant that orange trees looked as if they were covered with snow. He reasoned that in Australia the population of this scale insect was kept at a low level by a predator or a parasite that did not exist in California, and that this pest could be controlled in California by identifying the Australian predator or parasite and establishing it in California.

The whole story of the implementation of this biological control is long and complex, involving political as well as entomological problems. But in short, an American entomologist went to Australia; discovered the relevant predator, the vedalia ladybird; and brought several hundred of them home to California. They quickly became established, and by 1889 had all but eliminated the cottony cushion scale from the state. To this day, for well over a century, this scale insect has been controlled by the vedalia, small numbers of which coexist with a population of cottony cushion scales they keep low enough to be harmless.

Biological control is a mixed blessing. Nonnative parasites or predators introduced to control weeds or pest insects (usually also nonnative species) may attack organisms other than the target species. For example, from 1906 to 1986 a parasitic fly (*Compsilura*) from Europe was repeatedly released in North America to control the horribly pestiferous European gypsy moth. In the maggot stage the fly is an internal, lethal parasite not only of gypsy moth caterpillars but also of at least two hundred other kinds of caterpillars. Because of this parasite, reports George Boettner and his coauthors, populations of some of our native silk moths, the beautiful cecropia, our largest moth—with a wingspan of up to 6 inches—and the somewhat smaller but also beautiful promethea, have declined so much that their cocoons, once a common sight on trees and shrubs in winter, are now almost impossible to find. This is a shame, because many a child's first introduction to nature was watching one of these moths emerge from its cocoon—often in a grade school classroom.

The most endearing of the insects, cherished for their beauty, are surely the butterflies. In *An Obsession with Butterflies,* Sharman Apt Russell reminisces about the first time she really noticed a butterfly, a large tiger swallowtail that "dipped" by her face. "Its lemon yellow wings were striped improbably and fluted in black. They filliped into a long forked tail with spots of red and blue. . . . The butterfly floated away, leaving me pleased and agitated, as though I had been handed a gift I didn't deserve."

In diverse cultures in different parts of the world, butterflies have been thought to be symbols of the souls of the dead, or even the incarnation of the souls themselves. In Greek, for example, *psyche* means both butterfly and soul, spirit, or mind. The goddess Psyche was often represented as a butterfly by the ancient Greeks, symbolizing rebirth and life after death, according to Charles Hogue. Just as the beautiful butterfly emerges from the motionless and apparently dead pupa (chrysalis), the soul leaves the corpse. In Christian Europe, Hogue writes, "butterfly or moth wings occasionally give powers of flight to some angelic forms and often to fairies and nymphs." In the Middle Ages, Russell tells us, "people believed that butterflies, or *buterfloeges,* were disguised fairies bent on stealing . . . butter, milk and cream."

In a striking parallel to ancient Greece, the Tarahumara Indians of Mexico, Peter Kevan and Robert Bye relate, believe that butterflies and moths symbolize birth and death and souls. When death occurs, a soul ascends into heaven by three stages. "At the final, highest level, the ... soul becomes ... (a *nakarówili ariwá,* 'soul moth') and returns to earth and is burnt to ashes when attracted to fires." In the Tarahumara language, the "word for soul and for breath, *iwigá* or *ariwá,* is similar to that for ... butterfly, *iwiki,* both probably with the common root, *iwi.*" The transformation of the soul to a butterfly is deeply rooted in the traditions of Central America. Archaeological evidence from ancient Teotihuacán, near Mexico City, demonstrates the Toltecs' belief in the transformation of the souls of their rulers and warriors to butterflies. Ronald Cherry recounts the myth that the powerful plumed serpent god of the Aztecs, Quetzalcoatl, "first enters the world in the shape of a chrysalis, out of which the god painfully emerges into the full light of perfection symbolized by the butterfly."

The late Miriam Rothschild, an eminent entomologist, was, like her father, a world authority on fleas, and she was a niece of Walter Rothschild, who was a world-renowned butterfly expert and the "Dear Lord Rothschild" to whom the Balfour Declaration (pledging the British government's support for creation of a Jewish homeland in Palestine) was addressed. She expressed her love for nature, and butterflies in particular: "I garden purely for pleasure. I love plants and flowers and green leaves, and I am incurably romantic, hankering after small stars spangling the grass. Butterflies add another dimension to the garden, for they are like dream flowers—childhood dreams—which have broken loose from their stalks and escaped into the sunshine."

Butterfly gardening is becoming ever more popular. Butterfly gardeners forgo horticultural varieties—which are most often nonnative species whose blossoms usually don't attract our native butterflies—to plant native wildflowers that are favored by our butterflies. Thirty of these plants, a small fraction of those available, are illustrated by Mary Booth and Melody Mackey Allen in a delightful and informative book on butterfly gardening. The blossoms of these plants, and those of many other native plants, rival or even exceed in beauty those of many conventional horticultural varieties. Among them are the butterfly weed, with its large masses of bright orange florets; the daisylike violet flowers of the lovely New England aster; the tall joe-pye weed's large heads composed of small rose-colored florets; bee balm, a mint with clusters of bright red florets; and the yellow goldenrods, so beautiful that they are cultivated in England, where they do not occur naturally and are not taken for granted as they are in North America.

Never will I forget the breathtaking beauty of the first morpho butterfly I saw in the wild—in a tropical forest along a river not far from Ciudad Mante, Mexico. It was my first visit to the tropics. I was enthralled! There were birds I had never before seen: white-collared swifts swooping over the river, flocks of noisy red-crowned parrots, a colorful coppery-tailed trogon perched in a tree. But although I was and still am a compulsive bird watcher, seeing that one morpho flitting between the trees was the most memorable event of the day. I had seen dead morphos pinned in collections, but this living, moving, beautiful creature blew my mind. It was the biggest butterfly I had ever seen. The upper surface of the wings was a blazing iridescent azure blue, like a piece of sky that flashed as the morpho leisurely flapped its wings.

I caught the morpho in my net—ultimately for a good cause: it would eventually be added to the Illinois Natural History Survey's insect collection, a nationally important scientific resource. But actually, I caught it because I just had to possess this incredibly gorgeous specimen. When I had the morpho in my hand, I saw that when the light hit the wings at one angle the blue iridescence gleamed, but at another angle the wings looked black.

Obviously, its blue color is not a pigment, like the red of strawberries whose juice stains our fingers. But, then, what is it and how is it produced?

The Splendor of Iridescence by Hilda Simon gives a long and detailed but reader-friendly and sometimes lyrical explanation of iridescence—and also lovely color paintings of morphos. The wings of a butterfly or a moth (both belong to the order Lepidoptera, the "scale wings") are actually membranous and transparent. The color is provided by tiny scales that cover the entire wing both above and below, overlapping like shingles on a roof. These scales, which are generally pigmented, are the colored "powder" that sticks to our fingers when we handle a moth or a butterfly. But how is it that the unpigmented scales on a morpho's wings can be an iridescent blue? A rainbow or a prism shows us that white light is composed of all the colors of the rainbow. As Simon explains, however, the morpho's iridescent scales reflect only the blue because they are traversed by many thin, microscopic ridges with light-reflecting surfaces spaced at intervals about equal to the wavelength of blue light. If the light hits the scale at a certain angle, a color, blue in this case, is reflected if its wavelength is in phase with the spacing of the ridges. The reflections of colors that are out of phase cancel each other out, and thus from other angles the wing looks black.

Some think that science has drained nature of its quality of wonder and enchantment. Not so. By looking beneath the surface, science reveals an even more wondrous and sometimes more awesome beauty. Understanding how the morpho's iridescence is produced enhances rather than detracts from our enchantment with the butterfly. Can we look with wonder on nature only if we are ignorant of its innermost secrets?

For thousands of years, the Japanese have admired and loved dragonflies and damselflies (order Odonata), but not everyone in the world likes them. In Britain and North America they were—until recently—generally ignored or sometimes even feared, although they are harmless. Frank Lutz wrote that they "have been called Devil's Darning-needles and accused of sewing up the ears of bad boys; Snake-doctors and Snake feeders on the theory that they administer to the needs of reptiles; and Horse-stingers on the equally mistaken notion that they sting." But the reputation of dragonflies has been steadily improving in North America. We will come back to that after considering the fondness of the Japanese for these beautiful insects.

In 1901, Lafcadio Hearn, then a lecturer on English literature at the Imperial University of Tokyo, wrote that "one of the old names of Japan is *Akitsushima,* meaning 'The Island of the Dragon-fly,' and is written with the character representing a dragonfly—which insect, now called *tombō,* was anciently called *akitsu.*" North Americans and Europeans have few traditional common names for their dragonflies, but the Japanese have endearing folk names for many of the two hundred species on their islands: *tonosama tombō,* august-lord dragonfly; *yanagi-jorō,* the lady of the weeping willow; *ta-no-kami-tombō,* dragonfly of the god of rice fields. "For more than ten centuries," noted Hearn, "the Japanese have been making verses about dragonflies; and the subject remains a favorite one even with the younger poets of today. The oldest extant poem about a dragon-fly is said to have been composed over fourteen hundred years ago by the Emperor Yūriaku. One day while the Emperor was hunting, say the ancient records, a gadfly came and bit his arm. Therewith a dragon-fly pounced upon that gadfly, and devoured it. Then the Emperor commanded his ministers to make an ode in praise of that dragon-fly."

The Japanese have written many *haiku,* poems of three lines, about dragonflies. Some of my favorites of those quoted by Hearn are:

Kaki-daké to
Tombō to Utsuru
Shōji Kana!

The shadow of the bamboo-fence, with a dragonfly at rest upon it, is thrown upon my paper-window.

Wata-tori no
Kasa ya tombō no
Hitotsu-Zutsu

Look at the bamboo hats of the cotton pickers! There is a dragon-fly perched on each of them.

Tombō no
Ha-ura ni sabishii,—
Aki-Shiguré

Lonesomely clings the dragon-fly to the underside of the leaf—Ah! The autumn rains!

The love for dragonflies persists in Japan. In Nakamura City, on the island of Shikoku, there is a modern museum devoted to dragonflies and their close relatives, the damselflies, and nearby is a dragonfly sanctuary established by the national dragonfly society.

Americans and Canadians have long appreciated the decorative qualities of dragonflies and damselflies. These graceful insects are a popular motif for jewelry, women's clothing, neckties, lampshades, umbrellas, and almost anything else. But only recently have North American people other than entomologists taken an interest in the living dragonflies themselves.

A few years ago, while birding in Algonquin Provincial Park in Ontario, I came upon a small group of people with binoculars. They were indeed birders, but on that day they were using close-focusing binoculars and identifying butterflies, making a survey of their populations. I knew about bird watchers watching butterflies, but I learned something new when they told me that the next day they would make a survey of dragonflies.

Sidney Dunkle's *Dragonflies through Binoculars* is a field guide to the dragonflies of North America, illustrated with more than 380 color photographs. Dunkle notes, "Practically no common names are used by the public for individual species of dragonflies. Thus this book uses English names, newly standardized by the Dragonfly Society of the Americas." There are other field guides to dragonflies and there are several other dragonfly societies: the International Dragonfly Society (FSIO, Foundation Societas Internationalis Odonatologica), with headquarters in the Netherlands; the Worldwide Dragonfly Association, headquartered in Germany; and state societies in Ohio and Michigan.

Early on a calm, pleasantly warm night in June, fellow bird watcher Myrna Deaton and I were parked beside a meadow in far southern Illinois. We were listening to night birds: whip-poor-wills and the occasional chuck-will's-widow clearly enunciating the calls for which they are named. Hundreds of fireflies, perhaps thousands, flashed on and off as they flew just above the grass in the meadow. For a few minutes we forgot the birds. Even Myrna, a more fanatical birder than I, was enraptured by the beauty of the dancing, sparkling little yellow lights.

As I explained to Myrna—probably telling her more than she wanted to know—these captivating insects are not flies. They are beetles. They generate light by a chemical reaction in an organ at the tip of the abdomen. It is a cold light, because the reaction is so efficient that nearly 100 percent of the energy it produces appears as light. In contrast, only 10 percent of the energy produced by an incandescent lightbulb is emitted as light, while a wasteful 90 percent is emitted as heat.

Children are captivated by fireflies; at least they were when I was a child. Like my little friends, I put them in a jar with some grass—we thought that's what they eat (they actually eat other insects)—and in my bed that night I watched them as they blinked in the dark. I once put a lot of fireflies in a jar to see if they would give enough light to read by. They actually did, but just barely enough and only if the type was large, and even then you strained your eyes. I wondered why only these insects, among the many others I saw, produced light and of what use it might be to them. Now I know, but I am still cheered by the first fireflies I see in June.

Yoko Muroga and Kazuko Sasamori explained to me that the Japanese are very aware of and fond of the luminous species of fireflies that occur on their islands. Their common name for these insects is *hotaru.* Lafcadio Hearn translated two Japanese children's songs about fireflies:

Hotaru koi midzu nomashō:
Achi no midzu wa nigai zo;
Kochi no midzu wa amai zo;
Amai hō é tondé koi!

Firefly, come hither, and you shall have water to drink!
Yonder the water is bitter;—here the water is sweet!
Come, fly this way, to the sweet side!

Hotaru, koi!
Tsuchi-mushi, koi!
Onoga hikari dé
Jō motté koi!

Firefly, come hither!
Glow-worm, come!
By your own light
Bring me a letter!

On my living room wall hangs a lovely framed example of Chinese calligraphy, the character for *firefly,* painted for me by my friend Mrs. Muroga. (The Japanese often use Chinese characters in their writing, particularly in scholarly and literary writing.) The lower part of the character is the sign for insects; rising from it are two graceful signs for flames. Hence, the literal meaning of the character is "fire insect."

Masako Yamamoto, a friend of Mrs. Sasamori, sent me her own prose translation of the lyrics of a graduation song, noting that in Japan this song used to be sung at the graduation ceremony in most schools. "Nowadays," she wrote, "some schools have adopted popular music instead of this song. My heart feels empty because I cannot think about a graduation ceremony without this song. I always played the piano accompaniment at the gradua-

Above: The Chinese character for this flashing male firefly has two parts, the symbol for insect below and the symbol for fire above.

tion when I was a music teacher in Japan." Here is Mrs. Yamamoto's translation of the lyrics:

> Throughout our school life, we studied very hard. In the old days, there were no lamps. During the summer, however, we could still study at night using the lights of fireflies that we collected in a cage. During the winter, we studied by the reflected light of piled snow through the window. Many years passed quickly without notice. Now, we are graduating from our school. We will open the door which is full of sweet (good old) memories, and we will part from each other. (Hopefully, we will see each other again.)

According to *Japan: An Illustrated Encyclopedia,* "The *hotaru,* firefly, has long been associated in Japan with the Chinese legend of a poor scholar who, unable to afford lamp oil, studied by the glow of the fireflies."

Firefly viewing (*hotarugari*), possibly introduced from China, has been popular in Japan for centuries. In 2006, the *Tokyo Sightseeing Comprehensive Guide* announced that the Twenty-sixth Iwakura Onsen Hotaru Matsuri (Firefly Festival) would take place from June 21 to July 15:

> Iwakura Onsen is a quaint hot spring village located in the north of Ome city. A lot of tourists visit the place wishing to see the fireflies during the "Hotaru Matsuri" period every year. The festival has been popular among people from long ago as a typical summer event. The lodging facilities arrange the transportation service by a shuttle bus to and from the firefly viewing spot for the guests. Other recommended attractions before and after the fantastic firefly viewing are Shiofune Kannonji Temple, hiking trails, [and a] hot spring spa known as the secret of beautiful skin!

The Chinese, too, have long been entranced by fireflies. Lafcadio Hearn translated from Chinese the following story from the *Sui Shu* (*Annals of the Dynasty of Sui*): "In the 12th year of Da Yeh (616), Emperor Yang visited the

Ching Hua Palace. Bushels of fireflies were collected by imperial order. In the evening, the Emperor and his courtiers went up the mountain. The fireflies were then released and the whole valley became immediately enlivened with the sparklings of these insects."

Isak Dinesen was as enamored of fireflies as we are. In *Out of Africa,* she wrote poetically on the beauty of the fireflies that, in the highlands of Kenya, begin to appear in the woods in early June, when the nights begin to be cold:

> On an evening you will see two or three of them, adventurous lonely stars floating in the clear air, rising and lowering, as if upon waves, or as if curtseying. To that rhythm of their flight they lighten and put out their diminutive lamps. The next night there are hundreds and hundreds in the woods.
>
> For some reason they keep within a certain height, four or five feet, above the ground. It is impossible then not to imagine that a whole crowd of children of six or seven years are running through the dark forest carrying candles, little sticks dipped in a magic fire, joyously jumping up and down, and gamboling as they run, and swinging their small pale torches merrily. The woods are filled with a wild frolicsome life, and it is all perfectly silent.

Entomologists have found some answers to the complex question of what use fireflies make of their ability to produce light. I used the word *some* advisedly. There is surely much more to be learned. But what we do know is wonderful. The flashing lights are signals between the sexes. The flying males flash a brief coded signal, much like Morse code, that is different from the signals of male fireflies of other species. If a female, perched on grass or other low vegetation, sees a male's signal and recognizes it as that of her own species, she responds by flashing a coded signal of her own. It may be quite different from the male's but is characteristic of her species, and he recognizes it. It reveals her location to him and tells him that she is a willing female of his own species.

He'd better be wary, however. There is another firefly in the ointment, so to speak. Some females' signals lure males to their deaths. Males of the *Photinus* genus of fireflies, those we have been considering thus far, are sometimes eaten by females of the *Photuris* genus of fireflies. These latter females respond to courting males of their own species with the appropriate flash signal. They mate with their own males and do not usually eat them. But their response to the signals of other firefly males is different. They respond to the flashes of *Photinus* males with the counterfeited flash signal of the *Photinus* female. The *Photuris* females have broken the *Photinus* code. These firefly femmes fatales, as they were dubbed by James E. Lloyd, who discovered this deception, devour the hapless *Photinus* males that they lure in with false signals. Females of some species of *Photuris* have an impressive repertoire. They can mimic the signals of several species of *Photinus*.

The glowing, flashing firefly trees of Southeast Asia are among the most striking and amazing of natural phenomena. Engelbert Kampfer's description, quoted by John Buck, of firefly trees he saw in what is now Thailand in the early eighteenth century is probably the first published description of this marvelous phenomenon: "The glowworms ... represent another shew, which settle on some trees like a fiery cloud, with this surprising circumstance, that a whole swarm of these insects, having taken possession of one Tree, and spread themselves over its branches sometimes hide their Light all at once, and a moment after make it appear again with the utmost regularity and exactness."

Tens of thousands of individuals rest in the tree during the day, but at night the males flash brightly in virtually perfect synchrony at, depending on the species, from half-second to 3-second intervals. Both sexes are attracted to the tree, but the females do not participate in the synchronous flashings. A female's dim glow is visible in the dark intervals between the male's flashes, however, probably informing the males that a willing sexual partner is nearby. Once they have been inseminated—probably by more than one male—they leave the tree to distribute their eggs in microhabitats suitable for their larval offspring.

I have heard that when a world-renowned authority on ants was approached by a woman who said that she had ants in her kitchen and asked what she should do, he told her to "step carefully." Very few would have advised such consideration for the ants. When they see ants in their home, most people call in an exterminator or, at far less cost and leaving behind almost no toxic residue, set out strategically placed toxic ant baits. Nevertheless, although they usually do not welcome them in their homes, people of many cultures admire ants as exemplars of industry and organized activity.

The proverbs of Solomon, the great king of Israel who lived about three thousand years ago, are preserved in the Bible. He advised the indolent person who does not look to the future:

Go to the ant, thou sluggard;
Consider her ways, and be wise:
Which having no chief,
Overseer or ruler,
Provideth her bread in the summer,
And gathereth her food in the harvest.
How long wilt thou sleep, O sluggard?
When wilt thou arise out of thy sleep?
(Proverbs 6:8–9)

About four hundred years later in Greece, Aesop told the fable of the grasshopper and the ants. The grasshopper approached a group of ants who were drying their store of seeds in the sun and begged them for a few seeds, complaining that he was starving. The busy ants stopped working briefly and asked the grasshopper why he had not collected a store of food to tide him over the winter. The grasshopper explained that he had been too busy singing. (Aesop probably did not know that the male grasshopper had been singing to attract a mate, and that, although both would soon die, their progeny would survive the winter as eggs buried in the soil.)

In the second century C.E., about eight hundred years after Aesop, the Latin writer Apuleius told the story of how Psyche, a mortal, became an immortal goddess. Because the story, beautifully told by Edith Hamilton, is long and complicated, I will cut to the role of the ants. The goddess Venus, jealous of Psyche's beauty, sets her a series of impossible tasks. For the first task, she presents Psyche with a large heap of mixed small seeds of many different kinds and tells her that she must have them sorted by nightfall. The ants, "the tiniest creatures of the field," come to Psyche's aid. "They labored separating and dividing, until what had been a confused mass lay all ordered, every seed with its kind."

Samuel Johnson, the English lexicographer and writer, penned the following poem:

Turn on the prudent ant thy heedless eyes,
Observe her labors, sluggard! and be wise.
No stern command, no monitoring voice,
Prescribes her duties or directs her choice;
Yet timely provident she hastes away,
To snatch the blessings of a plenteous day;

When fruitful summer loads the teeming plain,
She crops the harvest, and she stores the grain.

Some insects are liked or appreciated only under particular circumstances or by people with specialized interests. For example, even one of our most destructive insect pests, the infamous cotton boll weevil, eventually came to have a few grudging appreciators of its role in history. These beetles invaded Texas from Mexico in 1892, and by 1922 had infested most of the cotton belt of the southeastern states, destroying cotton buds, flowers, and bolls. It was a catastrophe! The cotton boll weevil became the most feared and hated insect in the South. Tom Turpin quotes a verse from a song popular at the time:

The boll weevil ate half the cotton,
And the banker got the rest;
Didn't leave the farmer's wife
But one old cotton dress,
And it was full of holes, and it was full of holes.

In 1915, after the boll weevil arrived in Coffee County, Alabama, the county's economy was at a standstill. The weevil had destroyed 90 percent of the cotton crop, and cotton had been virtually the whole foundation of the economy of this county and much of the rest of the cotton belt. The farmers responded by planting other cash crops. These included peanuts, for which George Washington Carver of the Tuskegee Institute in Alabama had found a multitude of uses and which he had been recommending to southern farmers for decades.

The switch to diversified farming was a godsend, and some saw the silver lining in the dark cloud of the weevil's devastation. In the center of Enterprise, Coffee County's largest town, stands a monument erected in 1919 to memorialize the boll weevil's role in diversifying the economy. An inscription on the statue reads: "In profound appreciation of the Boll Weevil and what it has done as the herald of prosperity." It would have been more appropriate to erect a statue of Carver, but honoring a black man in the South of the early twentieth century would have been all but unthinkable.

Very few people like fleas, but even these bloodsuckers once had, in the sixteenth and seventeenth centuries, an envious following that consisted only of men. In those days sanitation was at best cursory, and fleas were common in homes and on people's bodies—even on the prominent ladies who held fashionable salons attended by artists, writers, and other notables. In the late sixteenth century, Madeleine des Roches and her stepdaughter Catherine held such salons in Poitiers, France. During a gathering in 1579, a flea appeared on the bosom of the nubile and lovely Catherine. The gentlemen who were present were enchanted and wrote poems to commemorate the event. Étienne Pasquier, a minor French poet, wrote with envy of the fortunate flea that bit the soft flesh between the swelling breasts of the beautiful Catherine. These poems belong to a genre of flea-on-bosom poetry that actually began in antiquity, continued well into the nineteenth century, and even now is echoed in limericks and jokes. Like Pasquier's, many of these verses express envy of the flea, and others make more or less risqué speculations on what part of the woman's anatomy the flea might visit next.

Early in the seventeenth century, the English poet John Donne wrote a wistful poem, "The Flea":

> Marke but this flea, and marke in this,
> How little that which thou deny'st me is;
> It suck'd me first, and now sucks thee,
> And in this flea, our two bloods mingled bee;

Thou know'st that this cannot be said
A sinne, nor shame, nor losse of maidenhead,
Yet this enjoyes before it wooe,
And pamper'd swells with one blood made of two,
And this, alas, is more than wee would doe.

A risqué joke about two fleas that lived on the body of a voluptuous young woman was going around when I was an undergraduate: One day, as night was falling, the fleas went their separate ways to find cozy places to sleep. When they met the next morning, they asked each other if they had found comfortable shelters. One said that it had slept in a deep valley between two large, round mountains. The other had wandered into a dense and tangled forest and had slept in a cozy shelter that I had better not mention.

Some country folk and at least one television weather forecaster in Champaign, Illinois, believe that the amount of black in the hairy coat of the wooly bear caterpillar, the larva of the tiger moth, forecasts the severity of the coming winter. These fuzzy caterpillars, somewhat over 2 inches long, clothed with black bristles on both ends and reddish brown bristles in the middle, are commonly seen crawling across roads with obvious haste on warm days in late autumn. According to John Henry Comstock, the father of academic entomology in the United States, the behavior of these caterpillars inspired the New England metaphor "hurrying along like a caterpillar in the fall." Those who believe that these caterpillars can predict the weather months in advance keep an eye on them and even send specimens to the Champaign weather forecaster. But Comstock points out that "the extent of the black color varies in different individuals," and Lorus and Margery Milne explain that its coloration actually "indicates how near the caterpillar is to full growth before autumn weather stimulates it to seek a winter shelter."

I doubt that the wooly bear is stimulated to seek shelter only by the autumn weather. Like many other insects, it probably heeds the most reliable indicator of the seasons, the length of the day, which begins to decrease after June 22, the longest day of the year, and then begins to increase after December 22, the shortest day of the year. The short days of autumn stimulate a wooly bear to seek shelter, just as they trigger the blossoming of chrysanthemums and your Christmas cactus. If it survives the winter, the partly grown wooly bear resumes feeding for a while in spring and then spins a cocoon composed of its hair bound together with silk. It soon emerges from the cocoon as an adult moth with yellowish wings sparsely dotted with black spots.

My eye doctor asked me to help him find copies of three out-of-print publications of the Illinois Natural History Survey, lengthy technical monographs on mayflies, stoneflies, and caddisflies. These aquatic insects are likely to live in rocky, fast-flowing streams: trout waters. He was, of course, a fisherman who angled for trout with artificial lures known as "flies," fish hooks adorned with feathers and fur so that they resemble aquatic insects. Many who fish for trout, my ophthalmologist among them, are purists who disdain worms and other live bait, and fish only with flies. To quote Charles Waterman's *A History of Angling,* "I like to fool the trout myself. God makes aquatic insects. I make flies." The ultrapurists know quite a bit of entomology. They can identify many aquatic insects, understand their life cycles, and know at what time of year they emerge from the water as adults—all with a view to deceiving trout by tying flies that look like specific aquatic insects and by knowing when and where to use them.

For example, immature mayflies, nymphs, cling to rocks in streams or even hide under them until they are full grown. Then—each species in its own season—they swim to the surface and briefly stand on the surface film as they molt to the winged adult stage and then fly off to mate and lay eggs. Trout are wary and most likely to be caught by casting flies that resemble the species and life stage of a mayfly that is in season. In the early stages of a hatch, trout can be fooled with a "wet fly" that sinks, resembles the appropriate nymph, and is retrieved so as to imitate the movements of a swimming nymph. Later, as the hatch proceeds, "dry flies," which do not sink and look like a newly emerged adult mayfly of the same species resting on the surface film, are cast so that they land on the surface lightly, so as not to alert the trout to the deception.

Fly fishing has ancient roots. Larry Koller quotes the Roman Claudius Aelian's observations of angling in Macedonia made more than seventeen hundred years ago: "They fasten red wool around a hook and fix to the wool two feathers that grow under a cock's wattles, and which in color are like wax. The rod they use is six feet long and the line of the same length. Then the angler lets fall his lure. The fish, attracted by its color and excited, draws close and . . . forthwith opens its mouth, but is caught by the hook, and bitter indeed is the feast it enjoys, inasmuch as it is captured."

In 1653, Izaak Walton published what is probably the most widely known book on angling, *The Compleat Angler or the Contemplative Man's Recreation.* As Waterman puts it with some disdain, "Walton was a bait soaker." That is, he used worms and other live bait. But Charles Cotton, a coauthor of later editions of *The Compleat Angler,* was not just "a bait soaker" and added a list of many artificial flies and described in detail the methods of tying flies. Fly fishing has evolved to the point that it is almost a religion with some people who angle for trout. "No other form of angling," writes Waterman, "has been so surrounded by ethics, 'codes' and even formality."

But there are still those who, although the practice is disdained by fly casters, fish for trout with live bait. When I was growing up in Connecticut, my friends and I were among them. We used earthworms, not aquatic insects. In nature, trout find worms when a dirt bank falls into a stream. We had figured this out and primed the trout for a meal of worms by kicking soil into the stream. Then we ran downstream and put our bait into the water when the soil came drifting by. We didn't know that it was bad form to use live bait. We weren't trying to deceive the fish. We just wanted to catch and eat them.

In modern times, flies are attached to the fishing line by a "leader," a long, thin, and transparent length of a synthetic fiber such as nylon, but for centuries before the synthetics became available, leaders were made from natural silk in a very unusual way. According to Richard Peigler, silk glands were removed from mature caterpillars before they began to spin a cocoon. This was not the famous silkworm of commerce that you will meet in the next chapter, but a Chinese species of giant silkworm related to the common promethea and cecropia moths of North America. The silk glands—containing not-yet-hardened silk—were "soaked in vinegar, washed, [and] stretched more than 2 [yards]." This industry was practiced primarily on the Chinese island of Hainan in Guandong province.

The next chapter considers an insect, the silkworm of commerce, that is materially beneficial to people because it produces an extremely valuable product, silk fibers, which are woven into luxurious textiles. In later chapters we will discover that other insects are valued by people because, in one way or another, we make use of their bodies or, as with the silkworm, of a product that they produce.

11 The Silk We Wear

Many thousands of years ago, the Chinese learned to weave a marvelous cloth from thin silken threads secreted by the salivary glands of an insect—the mulberry silkworm, a caterpillar, the larval stage of the silk moth (*Bombyx mori*). Like many other insects, silk moth caterpillars use these threads to spin a silken cocoon in which they will molt to the pupa, the transformation stage, in which they metamorphose from the wormlike larval stage to the winged adult stage. Despite its "lowly" origin in the viscera of a mere insect, people all over the world have always loved and greatly prized silk.

It is said that in the year 2640 B.C.E. the Chinese empress Hsi-ling Shih accidentally dropped a silkworm cocoon into a cup of hot tea. As she retrieved the cocoon, she unraveled an extremely long, thin thread from it. (Later we will see why this was possible after, but not before, the cocoon had been immersed in hot water.) Some say that this was the origin of sericulture, the art of raising silkworms and harvesting their silk, but the discovery of silk cloth in ancient burials indicates that the usefulness of silk was discovered much earlier, possibly during the late Stone Age.

For thousands of years the Chinese jealously guarded their secret source of silk and the method of its production. By the first millennium B.C.E. they were trading silk cloth with India, Persia, and Turkistan. By the end of that millennium sericulture had spread to India and, a few hundred years later, to Japan. In the sixth century C.E., at the bidding of Justinian I, the emperor of Byzantium, two Persian monks smuggled silkworm eggs to Constantinople in their hollow canes. The Oriental secret was out! These few eggs were the foundation of European sericulture, which was to become a major industry, mainly in Italy and France. As we will see later, in the nineteenth century sericulture was attempted in the United States, but because Americans could not compete in this labor-intensive business with lower-paid foreign workers, it was soon abandoned.

There is no disputing that silk is the queen of fabrics. Silk cloth, writes Philippa Scott in an elegant, illuminating, and lavishly illustrated book, "is sumptuous, royal, heavenly; it is exotic, erotic, sensual. Most of all it is simply sheer beauty." Poets have acknowledged the qualities of silk. In the first century B.C.E., a poem by the Chinese emperor Han Wu-ti lamented that he no longer heard the rustling sounds of his dead mistress's silk skirt. When Shakespeare's Othello demands from Desdemona the fateful lost handkerchief, his first gift of love, he declares that it is endowed with supernatural virtues: "The worms were hallow'd that did breed the silk." In 1648, the English poet Robert Herrick wrote:

Whenas in silks my Julia goes,
Then, then, me thinks, how sweetly flows
That liquefaction of her clothes.

Next, when I cast mine eyes and see
That brave vibration each way free;
Oh how that glittering taketh me!

"There is no time in silk's history," Scott comments, "when it was not sought, valued, a symbol of the best, the most royal, the most holy, an honored gift." In twelfth-century Europe, bones and other holy relics of saints were paid homage by being wrapped in precious imported silk, often pieces of worn-out clerical vestments.

A person's importance in society has often been proclaimed by the opulence of the finery that he or she wears. And it is silk that is the hallmark of elegance and opulence. Mark Twain is reputed to have said: "Clothes make the man. Naked people have little or no influence on society." The *Dictionary of the Middle Ages* (edited by J. R. Strayer) is more explicit: "Clothes were social signatures. At a glance clothing informed an observer of the wearer's class, religion, particular craft or profession (and rank within it)."

Hundreds of years before Rome was founded in 753 B.C.E., the emperors of China wore garments of silk; by the time of the Manchu dynasty (1644–1912 C.E.) these had evolved into ceremonial robes that were ostentatiously ornate and extravagant creations of the finest silk brocades interwoven with gold threads. In the tenth century C.E., Murasaki Shikibu, quoted by Scott, gave an account of the role of silk clothing in the Japanese aristocracy of her day: "The garment was the person; it was the direct expression of his or her personality." In Chaucer's *Canterbury Tales,* written in Middle English in the fourteenth century and translated into modern English by J. U. Nicolson, the young and beautiful wife of the carpenter in the miller's tale is adorned with silk:

> A girdle wore she, barred and striped, of silk.
> An apron, too, as white as morning milk
> About her loins, and full of many a gore;
> White was her smock, embroidered all before
> And even behind, her collar round about,

> Of coal-black silk, on both sides, in and out;
> The strings of the white cap upon her head
> Were, like her collar, black silk worked with thread;
> Her fillet was of wide silk worn full high.

As it was in China, Japan, and later the Middle East, silk became the queen of fabrics in medieval Europe and was the ultimate in opulent dress. In certain countries and at certain times, sumptuary laws specified what medieval Europeans were allowed to wear. Sometimes their intent was to admonish people to eschew opulence, but more often they were meant to clearly distinguish social classes by their garments. For example, in 1488, according to John Vincent, women of Zurich, Switzerland, who were not of the aristocratic guilds were forbidden to wear "silk garments or silk trimmings on coats, shoes, neckcloths, and such." A 1693 ordinance in Nuremberg, Germany, advised women of noble families that "for bosom pieces they may use good velvet, damask, as well as silk goods worked in with silver and gold." But those of the trade and merchant classes were allowed to wear only breeches and jackets "of damask and inferior silk material, but satin, good figured velvet, cut or uncut, are totally forbidden under penalty of ten *gulden.*"

Amazingly enough, before the Spanish Conquest there were, according to Gary Ross, similar sumptuary laws among the Indians in what is now Mexico and in other parts of Middle America. "On all occasions," he stated, "from workaday labors to formal settings, even on battlefields, each individual wore fabrics that signaled his or her social status; dress was identity itself." Ross noted that dyes—natural dyes, of course—"were the principal basis of this hierarchy of clothing." In chapter 3, we will consider some of these natural dyes that were made from insects.

Despite nylon and the other synthetics, silk is still considered the most luxurious and glamorous of fabrics. In 1938, Brenda Frazier, the most famous debutante of the time, wore a trend-setting strapless gown of silk satin to her coming-out party. Haute couture designer Yves St. Laurent's revealing see-through blouse of silk chiffon created a sensation in 1966. The spring 2005 issue of *Weddings in Style* gave, in an article by Rory Evans titled "Trump and Circumstance," "an inside look at the mega-swank merger of Donald Trump and Melania Knauss." The bride's Christian Dior haute couture gown was made of 60 pounds of hand-beaded and embroidered white silk satin and valued at more than one hundred thousand dollars.

You may not know that many different groups of insects other than silkworms and their many caterpillar cousins—and also the spiders—have evolved the ability to synthesize and secrete silk. Silkworms and these other insects and the spiders do not, of course, produce silk just to please people. What use, then, do these hundreds of thousands of creatures—among the 900,000 known insect species and 65,000 known spiders and their relatives—make of the silk they produce? In his authoritative book on insect physiology, Sir Vincent Wigglesworth tells us how silk serves these creatures in the struggle to survive and reproduce. Furthermore, he points out that these various groups of insects use different organs to make silk, indicating that this very useful ability evolved independently several times.

Silkworms, many other moth and a few butterfly caterpillars, the larvae of wasps, ants, bumblebees, and other bees, and some other insects use silk secreted by the modified paired salivary glands and extruded by "spinnerets" on either side of the mouth to spin cocoons that protect them from the elements and from insect-eating creatures after they molt to the immobile and helpless pupal stage. Colonies of tent caterpillars shelter in large, white, and very conspicuous nests that they weave of silk secreted by their salivary glands in the crotches of wild cherry trees. In Asia and Africa, adult weaver ants, which cannot themselves secrete silk, build nests in trees by binding together leaves with silk produced by their larvae, which they hold in their jaws and use as weaving shuttles. Tiny, newly hatched caterpillars of gypsy moths and other moths—and spiders, too—may travel long distances, even many miles, as they float on the breeze suspended from long threads of silk. One of my graduate students, Aubrey Scarbrough, observed that cecropia caterpillars searching for a place in which to spin a cocoon mark their trail, which may be 30 or more feet long and which they may have to retrace, by laying down a single strand of silk on the trunk of their host tree and on the ground.

Much like many of the spiders, some insects use webs of silk to trap their food. For example, some stream-dwelling caddisfly larvae strain single-celled algae and tiny creatures from flowing water with nets of silk produced by their modified salivary glands. Boatloads of tourists, wrote Harold Oldroyd, visit Waitoma Cave in New Zealand to view huge colonies of "glowworms"—actually larval flies, midges—that suspend strands of silk secreted by their salivary glands from the cave ceiling. These strands are dotted with beadlike sticky globs that glow in the dark, attracting and trapping small flying insects. Other midge larvae dig U-shaped burrows in the bottom muck of lakes, blocking their front ends with silken nets. The net traps food particles from a current that the larva's undulations cause to flow from the rear to the front end of the tunnel. Every three to four minutes the midge larva eats the net and the food adhering to it and then spins a new net.

Male dance flies court females with a gift of food, an insect that some species wrap in silk secreted by glands in their front feet. Males of some other species of dance flies offer females nothing more than a large silken balloon that does not contain an insect. For reasons not known, the females mate with the males after accepting the balloon, a mere symbol of a gift of food.

The tiny insects known as web spinners (order Embioptera) live in galleries in the soil and other places that are lined with silk secreted by glands in their front feet. Unlike other insects, adult web spinners—not only the immature stages—can secrete silk.

The primitive, wingless silverfish do not practice internal fertilization. That is, the male silverfish, unlike other insects, does not have a functional "penis" to inject his sperm into the female's "vagina." A male silverfish deposits a packet of sperm on the ground and, to guide his mate to it, strings threads of silk, secreted by a penislike organ, that lead to the sperm packet. It is up to the female to follow the guiding threads and to find the packet of sperm and stuff it into her genital opening.

Lacewings, the adult form of the predaceous larvae known as aphid lions, lay loose clusters of eggs, but protect each egg from predators—as likely as not to be its newly hatched siblings—by placing it atop a tall, thin stalk of silk discharged from the anus and secreted by the Malpighian tubes, the insects' equivalent of kidneys. (The eighteenth-century Italian scientist Marcello Malpighi, renowned for his pioneering studies on human and insect anatomy, first described the structure and function of "insect kidneys" in his study of the anatomy of the silkworm.) Certain aquatic beetles enclose their eggs in a floating cocoon of silk, with a mastlike air intake, secreted by glands associated with the genitalia.

Over the millennia, silkworms, which no longer exist in the wild, have become so completely domesticated that, unlike any other insect—including even the honey bee—they are completely dependent on humans for food and care. The growing caterpillars are so "tame" and loath to move that, even when food is not available to them, they do not wander away from the open trays or shelves on which they are raised.

Silkworms are, as entomologists say, host plant–specific. That is, they would rather starve to death than feed on any plant other than the white mulberry, or less enthusiastically and with inferior results, on just a few of the other plants of the mulberry family. Such specificity is not unusual. Louis Schoonhoven and his coauthors estimate that about 80 percent of the four hundred thousand known species of plant-feeding insects are similarly picky eaters, willing to feed on a limited number of plants of only one or a few closely related families.

Marjorie Senechal, a professor at Smith College in Northampton, Massachusetts, and leader of a project to uncover the long history of sericul-

Above: A silkworm caterpillar munches on a mulberry leaf and a silkworm moth clings to the cocoon from which it has just emerged.

ture in Northampton, quoted from the minutes of an 1842 meeting of the New England Silk Convention: "*Resolved:* that, inasmuch as in America and China the mulberry tree is found in the native forests, it is a manifest indication of Divine Providence, that this country, as well as China, was designed to be a great silk growing country." But the many attempts to raise silkworms in the United States were ultimately abandoned. Perhaps the author of the resolution misread Divine Providence because his botany was weak. The same species of mulberry tree does *not* grow in the native forests of both America and China. The silkworm's favorite food, the white mulberry (*Morus alba*), a native of Eurasia, did not grow in America until it was imported to feed silkworms. The red mulberry (*Morus rubra*) is a native of American forests, but is an inferior food for silkworms, although people find its berries tarter and tastier than the usually insipid berries of the white mulberry.

Beginning with the earliest settlements in what was to become the United States, the establishment of an American silk industry remained a persistent goal for well over two hundred years. In 1607, notes Senechal, King James I of England sent the settlers of the new colony of Jamestown, Virginia, "eggs from his own private stock and copies for each . . . household of *A Treatise of the Art of Making Silk.*" According to Senechal, "silkworms were raised, with sporadic success, in every colony but Maryland." Attempts to raise silkworms in the United States persisted well into the nineteenth century, but all ultimately failed because sericulture is so extremely labor intensive. We learn from Senechal that silkworms were first raised in Northampton in the 1820s, when it "clacked with the sound of silkworms chomping mulberry leaves, and the Hampshire, Franklin, and Hampden Agricultural Fair awarded prizes for home-grown silk." By 1832, mills had been built and "silk was raised from moth to cloth." By 1846 the raising of silkworms had been abandoned, but the manufacture of the famous Corticelli and Nonotuck brands of thread continued, using silk imported from abroad. But by 1936, because of the Great Depression and competition from the increasingly popular rayon, the mills had been shut down forever.

Just how much labor is required to raise silkworms is made clear by Henrietta Aiken Kelly's U.S. Department of Agriculture bulletin, a set of "practical instructions" for sericulturists. Methods of maintaining a silkworm culture have changed with extensive advances in technology, but the basic process remains the same as in 1903, when Kelly wrote the bulletin.

According to Kelly, during the thirty to forty days in which silkworms grow from tiny hatchlings to full-grown caterpillars ready to spin cocoons, they increase in weight by an astounding fourteen thousand times. It is no wonder that these caterpillars have huge appetites. Kelly tells us that the silkworms that hatch from one ounce of eggs—a rather modest brood of forty thousand (give or take a few thousand) larvae—will eat a total of about 2,300 pounds, well over a ton, of freshly picked mulberry leaves. If well cared for, the caterpillars will convert this huge mass of leaves into about 170 pounds of silk.

As they pass through the five subdivisions (ages, or instars) of the larval stage—demarcated by four molts of the larval skin—the silkworms' appetites keep pace with their extraordinary growth rate, increasing at an astonishing exponential rate, surprising to the neophyte hobbyist who raises and feeds silkworms for the first time and must keep up with their extraordinary demand for mulberry leaves. During the first two ages, they eat only about 0.5 percent of their total food intake; in the third age, another 2.6 percent; in the fourth another 12 percent; and in the fifth and final age, a whopping 85 percent.

During the first age, Kelly observes, the tiny, newly hatched caterpillars are fed frequently by sprinkling finely minced, tender young mulberry leaves over them. Caterpillars of the second age are also fed finely minced leaves, but by the third age they are large enough to eat whole or coarsely cut leaves. During the fourth and fifth ages, they are given small branches bearing leaves. Beginning at the end of the first age, the caterpillars are presented with their food in an ingenious way that allows the sericulturist to discard the mass of leaf fragments and fecal pellets that accumulate under them. This mass of waste, "the bed," writes Kelly, "is, perhaps, the greatest source of danger to the worms. When there is not a free circulation of air, gases are developed which almost always cause fermentation, paving the way for future disease." When a cohort of caterpillars is ready to molt to the next age—normally in unison—their meals are presented to them on nets. Kelly explains the procedure:

> Place the last meal at night on the nets and extend them over the worms. By morning the worms will have mounted above the opening[s] in search of fresh leaf. Then lift up the nets, beginning at the top shelf [of a rack], and place them [and the silkworms] on clean shelves. Carefully detach from the nets any portion of the old bed.... The change of beds is thus rapidly effected with the least labor. It is very important that the tension of the net be such as to prevent the worms from being crowded together in the middle.

During the first five days of the fifth age, the worms grow enormously and it is very difficult to satisfy their immense appetite. During the next three days the caterpillars stop eating, but instead of scarcely moving except to find food, Kelly writes, they run "about in every direction, stopping from time to time and moving [their] head[s] like a blind person seeking the way. These signs indicate that the worm is looking for a convenient place to spin its cocoon." At that time loose bundles of brush or straw are placed on the shelves near the caterpillars, which climb up on them and spin their co-

coons of one long fiber of silk. Seven to ten days later, the caterpillars will have finished spinning, and the cocoons will be ready to harvest, have their loose excess floss removed, and heated to kill the pupae in the cocoons. If they are not killed, the moths will emerge from the pupae and exit from the cocoon through a hole they make after weakening the silk with an enzyme. This makes many breaks in the strand of silk, making it impossible to unwind as one continuous length the 1,200 to 1,600 yards of silk fiber of which the cocoon is spun.

A strand of silk, secreted by the paired silk glands, consists mainly of two filaments of a strong and elastic protein, fibroin, and also a sticky protein, sericin, that glues together these two filaments and also binds together the entire long strand of silk to form a sturdy shell, the cocoon. A silk strand cannot be unwound until the cocoon has been "softened" in hot water, removing the water-soluble sericin from the fibroin, which is insoluble in wa-

Above: In India, a woman tends almost full-grown silkworms eating their last meal of mulberry leaves.

ter. After a cocoon is softened, the loose end of the silk strand is caught, and then it and silk strands from several other cocoons are unwound and reeled together, forming a single length of strong thread.

Silkworms have benefited us not only as the source of fine fabrics; they have also been the laboratory animals, the central figures, in two major scientific discoveries, one of which had an immensely important impact on the practice of medicine—and another that added an entirely new dimension to our understanding of the behavior of insects, other animals, and even people.

"Toward the middle of the nineteenth century," writes René Dubos, "a mysterious disease began to attack the French silkworm nurseries. . . . By 1865, the silkworm industry was near ruin in France, and also, to a lesser degree, in the rest of Western Europe." Catastrophe loomed. Sericulture and the weaving of silk cloth had become a major part of France's economy. France's minister of agriculture appointed a team of scientists to study the disease. With "extraordinary foresight," Dubos writes, the eminent chemist and microbiologist Louis Pasteur was appointed to take charge of the team.

Pasteur was, indeed, the ideal person for the job. After three years of meticulous observation and experimentation, he discovered that there were actually two diseases and that both were caused by microorganisms, "germs," a different germ in each case. Silkworms infected with pebrine, a disease caused by a protozoan (a relative of the amoebas), are speckled with small black spots, suggesting the name *pebrine,* which means "pepper disease" in French. Most infected larvae grow slowly and remain very small; many die, and the survivors become weak and often deformed adults. Flacherie, from the French word for flaccid, is caused by a bacterium. Full-grown, seemingly healthy larvae become sluggish, vomit, have "diarrhea," and soon become limp, die, and turn black. Sometimes their flabby corpses droop from twigs in the bundle of brush provided for them as a spinning site. Once Pasteur knew the causes of these diseases, he figured out ways of preventing contagion and detecting diseased stock.

This was the very first demonstration that bacteria and other single-celled microorganisms cause diseases in animals (including humans). Several years earlier, Pasteur had predicted that germs would be found to be the cause of infectious diseases—the first statement of the germ theory of disease. He based this prediction on his research on fermentation and decay. It had been widely believed that the microscopic organisms so abundant in fermenting and decaying organic matter were spontaneously generated, the products of decay rather than its cause. He went on to demonstrate that spontaneous generation is impossible and that microorganisms, which are everywhere in the air, are without doubt the cause of fermentation and decay. As Dubos puts it, Pasteur then reasoned that "many of the other transformations of organic matter might also result from the activities of microbial life"—among them infectious diseases of animals and plants. Pasteur's proof that germs are the cause of diseases of silkworms was a watershed discovery, indisputable evidence that supported his germ theory of disease, one of the most important impacts, perhaps *the* most important, that biological science has had on the practice of medicine.

There were, of course, doubters who, using common sense, decided that the idea that invisible germs cause infections and disease was nonsense. Accordingly, they continued to perform amputations and other surgical procedures with unwashed hands and wearing aprons stained with the blood of previous patients. But the Scottish surgeon Joseph Lister, prompted by Pasteur's discoveries, began an educational crusade that eventually convinced the medical profession of the validity of the germ theory of disease. This not only made obvious the need for sterile surgical techniques but also led to the development of vaccines and to the discovery of the transmission patterns of other diseases: the transmission of influenza through the air; of bubonic plague, the black death, from rats to humans by fleas; of malaria from person to person by mosquitoes; and of Lyme disease from rodents to people by ticks.

The senses of taste and smell are as important to silkworms and other insects as vision and hearing are to us—perhaps even more so. Most insects find mates and otherwise communicate with others of their species by means of chemical signals called pheromones. Adult silk moths were the subjects of decades of research by the German chemist Adolf Butenandt that culminated in 1959 with the first isolation and chemical identification of a pheromone, the female silk moth's air-borne sex attractant.

The pheromone story began in 1874 when the French naturalist Jean-Henri Fabre, famous not only for his keen observations of insects but also for the literary merit of his books, made the astounding observation that a caged female peacock moth was attracting scores of males who were too far away to see her. How did she attract them? At first Fabre thought that she might be emitting "electric waves," but finally concluded that she was releasing a scent that people cannot smell but that male moths can—what we now call a pheromone. Not long after Fabre's observation, entomologists found that minute quantities of extracts of the "calling glands" of many female insects are powerful attractants for males. But these extracts were mixtures of many different chemical substances, and no one knew which one or combination of them was the actual attractant. And, needless to say, the chemical composition of not one sex attractant or other pheromone was then known. Unless its chemical composition is known, neither a pheromone nor any other chemical substance can be synthesized in the laboratory and thus be made available in large quantities for research and practical uses, such as baits to trap pest insects.

Although both male and female adult silk moths have wings, they cannot fly. Nevertheless, females emit a sex attractant pheromone that drives males into a sexual frenzy. Butenandt saw this as an opportunity to isolate and determine the chemical composition of the active component in a crude extract of a female silk moth's calling gland. He and his associates made extracts of the calling glands of about five hundred thousand female silk moths. From this large quantity of extract they isolated and determined the composition of a tiny amount of a substance, only 0.000042 ounce, that was as exciting to males, even in miniscule amounts, as the whole extract. This was the pheromone in its pure form, which Butenandt called bombykol.

Butenandt's discovery opened a floodgate. Entomologists and chemists have now, according to a Web site of the National Academy of Sciences, "broken the code for the pheromone communication of more than 1,600 insect species." We now know that there are many different kinds of pheromones, not only sex attractants. For example, ants daub the ground with a pheromone that marks the trail to a source of food; some insects, notably fruit flies, label a fruit in which they lay an egg with a pheromone that warns away other egg-laying females whose progeny would compete with theirs for food; and honey bees release into the air an alarm pheromone that incites their nest mates to sting and drive away bears, humans, or other honey thieves. Although pheromones were first discovered in insects, and most of the research on them has been with insects, we now know that animals other than insects, including, among many others, crabs, fish, dogs, and humans, use pheromones as a means of chemical communication.

Insect pheromones also have important practical applications. The use of mass-produced synthetic pheromones saves our economy hundreds of millions—if not billions—of dollars every year. For one thing, pheromones are used to monitor populations of pest insects. Pheromone-baited traps tell farmers and orchardists when a pest insect appears and whether or not the pests are numerous enough to make it economically worthwhile to apply an insecticide. In other words, will the monetary loss caused by the pest be more or less than the cost of applying the insecticide? Pheromones are also used to control pests. They can bait traps that kill males, thereby leaving many females unfertilized. Permeating a crop field or an orchard with a synthetic sex attractant makes it very difficult for males to locate females, thereby greatly limiting reproduction by a pest. According to the National Academy of Sciences Web site, pheromones used to disrupt mating in this way help to curb insect damage in orchards, vineyards, and tomato, rice, and cotton fields.

About 99 percent of the silk in world commerce, according to Richard Peigler, comes from the domesticated mulberry silk moth of the family Bombycidae. But he also lists more than twenty other moths and one butterfly, none of which feed on mulberry, that are now or were once sources of silk. Most are the "giant silk moths" of the family Saturniidae, which is related to the Bombycidae. (Some really are giants. Its maximum wingspan of 6 inches makes the beautiful cecropia one of North America's largest moths, and, with its 10-inch wingspan, the tropical Atlas moth, scientific name *Attacus*, is the world's largest moth.) Most of the other moths that are a source of silk are in the same family as the familiar North American tent caterpillar (family Lasiocampidae).

These two groups of moths use silk in two very different ways. Caterpillars of many of the giant silk moths spin silken cocoons, as does the mulberry silkworm, but often with leaves incorporated into the cocoon. The tent caterpillars, by contrast, whose silk is used in Mexico are primitively social—

"subsocial"—and live in large groups, cooperating to construct a communal shelter, a "tent," made of silk. Their shelters are much like those of the North American tent caterpillars, whose large, white nests shaped like upside-down pyramids are a familiar sight in the crotches of wild cherry saplings along country roads. With only a few exceptions, these cocoon- and tent-making moths are not reared in captivity. Their silk is collected in the wild.

Silk in the communal nests constructed by the subsocial caterpillars of certain moths and one butterfly cannot, of course, be reeled. The silk of *Gloveria psivii,* a Mexican relative of our tent caterpillar, is spun into thread after being plucked from nests that may be more than 3 feet long but are usually about half that long. Centuries before the invasion of Mexico by the Spanish conquistadores, *Gloveria* silk was used by the Aztecs and the Mixtecs and Zapotecs of the state of Oaxaca. According to Peigler, *Gloveria* silk was probably "an article of commerce" during the reign of the Aztec emperor Montezuma II, from 1502 to 1519, when he was deposed by the conquistadores. A very unusual butterfly that occurs in many parts of Mexico (you will hear more about it in chapter 6) is the only butterfly among the wild silkworms. Groups of the caterpillars cooperate to construct a nest of silk so dense and tightly woven that it was used by the ancient Mexicans like paper and, according to Peigler, was "collected and processed" in the Zapotec region as recently as the 1950s.

Years ago in Japan, my friend Yoko Muroga (whom you met in chapter 1) told me, small bags and sashes (obis) were made from the cocoonlike silken cases, bags, of the caterpillars known as bagworms. You have probably seen these cases, much like those that occur in Japan, hanging from the branches of an arborvitae, a blue spruce, or some other conifer. They attain a length of about 2 inches and are usually festooned with small plant fragments. In summer, they are the mobile shelters of voracious plant-eating caterpillars—

only their head and legs protruding from the bag. In winter, the bags made by females, larger than those of the males, contain hundreds of eggs and hang suspended from a branch by a strap of silk. In Japan, they were collected, stripped of plant fragments, and then slit open along one side, soaked in water to soften them, pressed flat, dried, and sewn together.

Some giant silk moth caterpillars, the American polyphemus and Asian members of the same genus (*Antherea*), make cocoons similar to those of the mulberry silkworm. The cocoon, spun in autumn, is a hollow shell composed of one long, unbroken strand of silk and has no valve, or escape hatch, for the moth that will emerge from it in spring. How, then, do these moths—and the mulberry silk moth—escape from the cocoons that imprison them? Fotis Kafatos and Carroll Williams found that a moth ready to emerge soaks the head end of the cocoon with a powerful enzyme that softens that part of the cocoon by "digesting" the sericin that binds together the strands of silk. Then, according to Paul Tuskes and his coauthors, the moth makes a large hole in the cocoon wall by tearing the silk filaments with hornlike projections, one at the "shoulder" of each wing. If the pupa is killed so that the cocoon will not be ruined by the moth's escape hatch, and if the cocoon is first dipped in hot water to dissolve the sericin, its silk can, like that of the mulberry silkworm, be reeled as a long, continuous strand.

The caterpillars of other giant silk moths, such as cynthia (*Samia cynthia*) and the eri silkworm (*Samia ricini*) of Asia and cecropia (*Hyalophora cecropia*) of North America, construct much more complex cocoons. They are double-walled and at one end have a valve through which the moth can escape. For example, my coworkers and I found that cecropia caterpillars first construct a tightly woven and tough outer wall (by weight, about 53 percent of the cocoon) that is attached along its length to a branch or twig or occasionally to some other surface. Next they spin a sturdy inner wall (42 percent by weight) suspended from the outer wall by a fluffy, sparse layer of silk strands (almost 5 percent by weight). Both the outer and inner walls have an emergence valve consisting of strands of silk pointing outward in a conical shape. The moth emerges from the cocoon by pushing these strands apart, but the valve, like a lobster trap in reverse, resists forced entry by intruders from the outside. Cocoons of the cynthia and promethea moths, which we will meet later, are similar but are suspended from a twig by a strap of silk. Cocoons with a valve cannot be reeled. Tufts of silk are pulled from them and spun into thread, as is cotton.

"Probably the most beautiful of all wild silk moths," writes Peigler, "is the ailanthus silk moth, commonly called the cynthia moth. . . . This insect is native to China, where its cocoons have been used for centuries to produce cloth, sometimes called fagara silk, and the practice continues today to a small degree." Cynthia caterpillars will reluctantly eat the leaves of many woody plants but seldom survive on any but those of the tree of heaven, *Ailanthus altissima.*

Cynthia, Edward Nolan reports, was first brought to the United States in 1861, prompted by enthusiastic reports from France of its potential as a silk producer. Caterpillars were released on ailanthus trees in Philadelphia. The moth quickly spread throughout the city, flourishing on both cultivated and wild ailanthus trees. Entrepreneurs interested in silk manufacturing brought it to other cities. Cynthia turned out to be a commercial failure, but by the late 1800s feral populations had become established in many cities of the northeastern United States.

The stage had been set for the establishment of these feral moths in 1820, when ailanthus—a native of Asia—was, according to Arthur Emerson and Clarence Weed, planted on Long Island, New York. It now grows in much of the continental United States. "Although the ailanthus is almost confined to cities," notes Kenneth Frank, "the tree flourishes in both urban and suburban areas, and occasionally rural areas." In cities it thrives in places where few other plants will grow, in what Frank describes as "uninviting industrial habitats." He writes, "Its distribution in Philadelphia today is typical of its urban pattern. It grows throughout the city, in cellar wells, poking up through iron grates in the sidewalk. Saplings sprout at the edges of parking lots and in cracks in the walls of old buildings."

The only feral cynthias I have seen were in Bridgeport, Connecticut. As I walked past a gloomy alley between a row of dilapidated buildings and a railway embankment in the winter of 1942, I glimpsed something odd in the alley. On closer inspection I saw that it was a cluster of pale beige—almost white—cocoons dangling from the bare branches of an ailanthus by thin, flexible cords, pedicels, as much as 2 feet long. The following spring, moths with 4-inch wingspans emerged from cocoons I had taken home. According to Frank Lutz's *Field Book of Insects,* they were cynthias. Neither Lutz's nor the other books I consulted over the years mention the spectacular 2-foot pedicels. But just a few weeks ago, I found in Henry McCook's 1886 *Tenants of an Old Farm* a drawing of cynthia cocoons with pedicels that long.

But why such long pedicels? Observations made by Jim Sternburg and me on another giant silk moth provide the answer. We found that, in winter, cocoons of the promethea moth dangle from thin wild cherry or sassafras twigs by flexible silk pedicels no more than an inch long. Before wrapping itself in a leaf to spin its cocoon, the caterpillar anchors the leaf to the woody twig from which it sprang by wrapping the inch-long leaf stem with silk and binding it to the twig. In this way, the cocoon and the pupa it protects are prevented from dropping to the ground with the leaf in autumn, where they would surely be prey for hungry mice. The pupa is also protected from birds, which rarely penetrate the dangling cocoon because it swings away when they peck at it.

Cynthia uses the same strategy to protect itself in winter when it is a helpless pupa in a cocoon. Because of the difference between the leaves of ailanthus and those of promethea's common host plants, however, cynthia has a much more difficult task. Cherry and sassafras have simple leaves, with just one blade and a short stem that attaches it to a woody twig. Ailanthus, on the other hand, has compound leaves, with a leaf stem that may be as much as 3 feet long, bearing two rows of opposite leaflets. In autumn, the tree sheds the entire compound leaf. Before spinning its cocoon, a cynthia caterpillar wraps itself in one of the leaflets rather than in a single simple leaf as does promethea. To keep its cocoon from falling to the ground in autumn, a cynthia caterpillar must wrap all of the leaf stem above its cocoon with silk and anchor it to the adjoining woody twig. But there's more to the story than that. In America, cynthia now has only one generation a year, but it originally had two. With wonderful parsimony, caterpillars of the first generation do not make a long pedicel as do their progeny, which will remain in their cocoons all through the winter. They spin a pedicel as short as promethea's, just long enough to attach the leaflet to the leaf stem, which will not be shed by the tree before the adult moth emerges later in summer. The descriptions and figures of cynthia cocoons with short pedicels were obviously based on the summer cocoons of the first generation, which no longer exists in the United States.

Once silk has been spun into thread and woven into cloth, it—like cloth made of cotton, wool, and other materials—is dyed. Until late in the nineteenth century, before synthetic dyes were produced, only natural dyes obtained from plants, insects, and even snails were available. But the very best and most highly prized of the red dyes was obtained only from the little cactus-feeding insect that you will meet in the next chapter: the sap-sucking cochineal.

III Dyeing the Cloth

The Aztecs were wearing ceremonial cloaks dyed a brilliant red when Hernán Cortés and the conquering Spanish invaders, who had come to steal gold from the Indians, confronted Montezuma and his nobles in the Aztec capital of Tenochtitlán (now Mexico City) in 1519. At that time, the Spaniards didn't know that the source of the beautiful red dye was the cochineal insect (from the Old Spanish *cochinilla,* a wood louse), or that it was destined to be the most prized red dye in the world for more than three centuries. As the story, which may be apocryphal, has it, they didn't recognize the source of the dye, the cochineal insects, when they first saw them. In the confiscated tribute paid to Montezuma by his enslaved people, they found not only the gold and silver they so greedily hungered for, but also small bags containing tiny dried insects, cochineals. At first they thought that these insects were lice, which were quite familiar to them and were certainly nothing to be prized. Frank Cowan quotes Torquemada (not the infamous Dominican priest of the Spanish Inquisition), who wrote of the confiscated tribute:

> During the abode of Montecusuma among the Spaniards . . . Alonzo de Ojeda one day espied . . . a number of small bags tied up. On opening one of them, what was his astonishment to find it quite full of Lice? Ojeda, greatly surprised at the discovery he had made, immediately communicated what he had seen to Cortes, . . . [and] informed him that the Mexicans had such a sense of their duty to pay tribute to their monarch, that the poorest and meanest of the inhabitants if they possessed nothing better to present to their king, daily cleaned their persons, and saved all the Lice they caught, and that when they had a good store of these, they laid them in bags at the feet of their monarch.

"We know," writes Donald Brand, "that cochineal dye was of some importance in preconquest Mexico as *nocheztli* [cochineal] cakes or tortas are listed as articles of tribute [to the Aztecs] in the *Matrícula de Tributos* and the *Codex Menducino.* Some 30 communities . . . in Oaxaca, Puebla, and Guerrero paid a tribute of many sacs or bags of nocheztli." The conquistadores, and the other Spaniards who soon followed them, commented enthusiastically on the range of colors of the fabrics in Mexican markets. "There was spun cotton in all colors, so that it seems quite like one of the silk markets of Granada." Greatly impressed with the Aztecs' wonderful red dye, the Spaniards were quick to investigate the nature and value of cochineal, which surpassed in the richness and beauty of its hue any other red dye known at the time. The first consignments of cochineal had arrived in Spain by 1523, and subsequently officers of the Crown in the New World, specifically including Cortés, "were ordered to inform themselves of the amount of dye produced and possibilities for the future." Dried cochineal insects became, per weight, second in value only to the precious metals. For more than three hundred years, from the early 1500s to the late 1800s, cochineal remained the most favored and precious of the red dyes. It would not surprise me to learn that

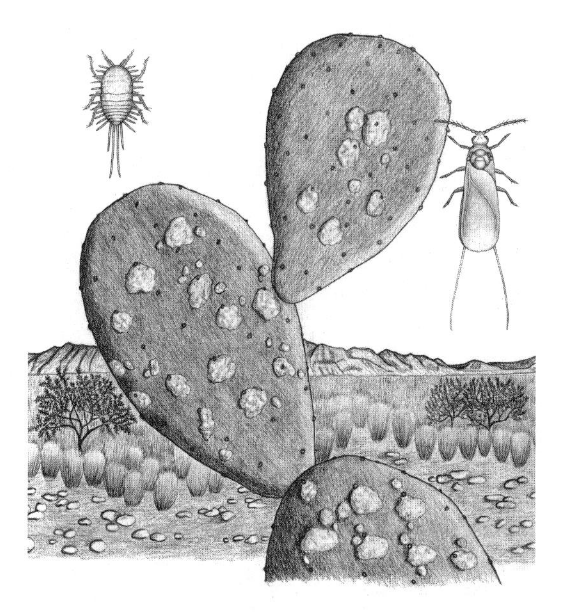

the value of the cochineal produced during those centuries exceeded that of all the gold and silver that the Spaniards stole from the native inhabitants of the New World.

The color red has a powerful effect on humans and other animals. It gets our attention. In the natural world, stinging or toxic insects protect themselves by warning birds of their noxiousness with their conspicuous coloration, very often red or a combination of red and black, as, for example, in ladybird beetles. Red stop signs and traffic lights along our streets warn us of danger. The maritime storm warning flag is a red banner with a black square at its

---

Above: Cochineals covered with white waxen threads on an Opuntia cactus; a newly hatched nymph is on the left and a winged male is on the right.

center. But in other contexts, red can be inviting. Many plants have red fruits, which attract the birds that will disperse their seeds by eating the fruit and eliminating the hard, indigestible seeds elsewhere, perhaps miles away. As for people, writes R.A. Donkin in his comprehensive monograph on cochineal: "Almost everywhere, red as the color of fire, the sun, and blood (and thereby life itself) has unusual significance, symbolizing magnanimity and fortitude, majesty, and power."

The cochineal insect (*Dactylopius coccus,* family Dactylopiidae) is actually, as John Henry Comstock tells us, a sap-sucking scale insect, superfamily Coccoidea, that, like the ground pearls we will meet later, is not, as are many of its relatives, armored with a hard scale that covers its body, although females do secrete filaments of white wax that cover their egg masses. The bright red, wingless mature females, rather large for a scale insect at a length of as much as a quarter of an inch, have weak legs and are barely capable of crawling. They release a scent, a sex pheromone, that attracts the winged males from a distance. (Adult cochineal males are the only winged individuals, as in any kind of scale insect.) After mating, the female lays a large batch of eggs, which she covers with white waxen filaments, and then dies. The newly hatched nymphs, known as crawlers, have strong legs and are very mobile; it is only in this stage, at the beginning of her life, that a female is likely to move about, but only over short distances. Like silkworms, cochineal insects are host plant–specific, fussy feeders that will live on and eat only certain species of prickly pear, or beaver tail, cactus (*Opuntia*).

There are some wild species of cochineal insects, but the domestic variety of the species that is grown commercially yields a superior dye. Growing and harvesting this insect was, as Charles Hogue tells us, most highly developed by the Aztecs in central Mexico and remained in their hands for many years after the conquest. The Spanish maintained a monopoly on the supply of cochineal for about 250 years—until late in the eighteenth century. During this period cochineal was produced only in the New World, mainly in Mexico and Guatemala. The Spanish not only kept the source of cochineal a "state secret," but also did nothing to dispel the misleading rumors that it was a plant product. Indeed, they fostered such tales. Samuel de Champlain, the French explorer who founded Quebec City, gave a supposedly firsthand description of cochineal's source in 1602. Champlain's description is a fantasy that owed everything to his imagination. According to his drawing and verbal description, quoted by Donkin, cochineal comes from a bushy plant that has "a fruit the size of a walnut which is full of seed within. It is left to come to maturity until the said seeds are dry, and then it is cut like corn and beaten to have the seed, of which they sow again so as to have more."

Although cochineal insects survive in the wild in Central and South America, the domesticated variety grown commercially probably could not survive without painstaking care from people. The first step in raising these insects is to establish a healthy plantation of prickly pear cactus, but only one of the few species of this large group of cacti on which this host-specific insect will feed should be planted. The plants require considerable care. They must be fertilized, weeded, protected from the depredations of other cactus-feeding insects, and prevented from growing taller than 4 feet, a height easily accessible to the workers who care for and harvest the cochineal insects.

At first the plantations were all small "Indian holdings," but by the eighteenth century there were also large plantations of sixty thousand or more plants. The methods for raising cochineal insects used on smallholdings were described by T. L. Phipson:

> The poor Indians . . . establish their nopal [prickly pear] plantations on cleared ground, on the slopes of mountains or ravines, two or three leagues from their villages, and when properly cleaned, the plants are in a condition to maintain the insects for three years. In spring, the proprietor of a plantation purchases as stock a few branches of . . . [prickly pear] laden with small cochineals recently hatched, called *semilla* (seeds). The branches may be bought for about three francs the hundred; they are kept for twenty days in the interior of the huts, and are then exposed to the open air under a shed, where, owing to their succulency, they continue to live for several months. In August and September the female insects big with young are gathered and strewn upon the nopals to breed. In about four months the first gathering, yielding twelve for one, may be made, which, in the course of the year, is succeeded by two more profitable harvests.

A different and more advanced method of raising cochineal insects is described by Donkin. Nevertheless, it still required much painstaking and finely exacting hand work. "Seeding" the plants, infesting them with the insects, was the first step. From ten to twenty-five gravid females were placed in a protective "nest" made of Spanish moss or some other plant fiber. Sometimes cloth bags were used, a practice later adopted by the cochineal farmers of the Canary Islands and the western Mediterranean coast. The females laid their eggs after the nest was attached to the plant, and the tiny, newly hatched insects crawled out of the nest, spread over the adjacent parts of the plant, embedded their sucking beaks in the tissues of the plant, and then remained completely immobile as they sucked sap and grew to maturity.

Only impregnated females were used to make the dye. Before they could lay their eggs, they were carefully removed from the plant, one by one, with a quill, a pointed twig, or a small brush; however, enough females to produce sufficient offspring for the next harvest were left on the plant. The harvested cochineal insects were then killed and dried by exposing them to the sun, which produced the finest dye, or by putting them in a heated room or an oven, which resulted in a somewhat inferior dye but was less time-consuming—a matter of hours rather than the week or more required for sun drying. The dried insects were shipped to market in Europe or occasionally the dye might be produced locally.

In pre-Hispanic Mexico, the annual tribute the Aztecs demanded from their conquered provinces included more than 9,000 pounds of dried cochineal insects. The demand for cochineal in the Old World was far greater than that, however. During Spain's 250-year monopoly on cochineal, vast quantities of these dried insects, raised in Mexico and Guatemala, were shipped to Spain and its Philippine colony. From there much of the cochineal was traded to other countries. In 1660, reports Donkin, 237,000 pounds were exported. But in the eighteenth century, these amounts were greatly exceeded: 875,000 pounds in 1736 and from 475,000 to 800,000 yearly between 1760 and 1772. A three-ship Spanish fleet that sank off the coast of Louisiana in 1776 is thought to have been carrying almost 600,000 pounds of cochineal, according to Gary Ross. It takes about seventy thousand dried cochineal insects to make a pound. Accordingly, that little Spanish fleet was carrying about forty-two billion of these insects. Just imagine the labor that went into rearing that many of these tiny creatures! It is no wonder that cochineal was and still is very expensive.

The Spanish monopoly was broken in 1777, when a naturalist surreptitiously entered Mexico, traveled on foot to Oaxaca, amazingly, and smuggled out cactus pads and cochineal insects. Phipson writes of this important incident: "A French naturalist, Thieri de Menonville, exposed himself to great dangers for the sake of observing and studying the cultivation of the cochineal in Mexico, in order to enrich by its means the Colony of St. Domingo. He carried there the two varieties [wild and domesticated] ..., along with the nopals on which they lived."

Once the secret was out, cochineal farming spread far and wide, first to Western Hemisphere countries such as Nicaragua, Colombia, Ecuador, Peru, and Brazil, and then to countries of the Old World, among them Algeria, India, and mainland Portugal and its Canary Islands, off the northwest coast of Africa. Phipson writes of the establishment of cochineal farming on Tenerife, one of the Canary Islands, early in the nineteenth century:

> Teneriffe had effectively been a vine-producing country for three hundred years; and when a gentleman introduced the cactus and cochineal there from Honduras, he was looked upon as an eccentric man, and his plantations were frequently destroyed at night. However, when the grape disease broke out,... [Tenerife] was gradually forsaken by vessels in quest of wine which could no longer be supplied; and with starvation staring them in the face, the inhabitants turned to cochineal growing: wherever a cactus was seen upon the island, a little bag of cochineal insects was immediately pinned to it. The essay succeeded admirably. An acre of the driest land planted with cactus was found to yield three hundred pounds of cochineal, and, under favourable circumstances, five hundred pounds, worth £75 to the grower. Such a profitable investment of land was never before made.

To keep up with the ever-increasing demand for this, then still the best and most beautiful of all the red dyes, the production of cochineal insects burgeoned. In 1858, Guatemala, then the leader in world production, exported about 2 million pounds. But by 1861, the center of cochineal production had shifted to the Old World. In that year, the Canary Islands alone exported more than 2.1 million pounds.

Late in the eighteenth century, Opuntia cacti and cochineal insects were brought to Australia in the hope of establishing a cochineal industry. That hope was never realized, but Opuntia was there to stay. It was planted as a garden flower, but it soon escaped from cultivation, flourished, and spread widely. By 1900 it had invaded close to 16,000 square miles of pastureland, an area about twice the size of New Jersey, and by 1925 it had overrun an area almost twelve times the size of New Jersey and was still on the move. All of this land was rendered practically useless, and about half of it was so overgrown with a thicket of these spiny plants that it was literally impenetrable to humans, cattle, sheep, and kangaroos. Where cacti grow naturally—only in the Western Hemisphere—nothing even approaching such a plague of these plants had ever been seen. Consequently, as Paul DeBach explains, Australian entomologists reasoned that Opuntia flourished so spectacularly in Australia because the insects that feed on cacti in the Western Hemisphere did not occur in Australia. Accordingly, cactus-feeding insects were imported from various parts of the New World. Among them were some species of cochineal insects, but by far the most effective of the introductions was the caterpillar of a South American moth with the appropriately descriptive scientific name of *Cactoblastis cactorum.* By 1937, the last dense stand of cactus in Australia had been whittled down to size by these insects. Today, the cacti in Australia—still controlled mainly by *Cactoblastis*—grow only in scattered clumps, and kangaroos, sheep, and cattle graze on once-useless land.

As recently as 1986, Gary Ross reports, a renowned master dyer and weaver in the village of Teotitlán del Valle in the state of Oaxaca, a Zapotec Indian named Isaac Vásquez, prepared cochineal dyes much as his ancestors had done long before the arrival of the Spanish in Mexico. In preparing the dye, Vásquez first crumbled dry leaves of the *tejute* tree into a cauldron of boiling water. The leaves probably act as a color intensifier and mordant—possibly, Ross proposed, because they contain oxalic acid, a known mordant, as do other plants closely related to *tejute.* (A mordant fixes a dye on cloth by combining with the dye to form a chemical compound that is insoluble in water.) In the meantime, Vásquez's wife, María, was grinding dried cochineal insects to a fine powder on a grinding stone, a *metate.* The next step was to add the ground insects and the juice of about eighty limes to the cauldron. "The Zapotec's use of lime, crucial for the intense red color, dates only to the sixteenth century," Ross reports. Vásquez's attempts to discover what acidic substance his ancestors used before the Spaniards introduced limes to the New World had been futile. He said, "The secret remains in a world we have lost." His final steps were to put skeins of wool, which María had spun by hand and then soaked in cold water, into the boiling cauldron and to stir thoroughly.

"Soon I understood," Ross writes, "why Isaac Vásquez is an internationally esteemed master of his craft." The color of the dyed wool depends on many factors: its initial color, which may range from white to nearly black, how long it remains in the dye bath, how much cochineal powder is used, and the amount and type of lime (dried or fresh) that is added to the dye vat. By manipulating these factors, Vásquez was able to create countless hues within the red spectrum. "Since the precise conditions are never recorded, however, only his years of experience and perceptive eye endow Isaac with a sensitive control of these natural colors." Vásquez makes good use of the wool he dyes. He is a master weaver whose tapestries, all woven of naturally dyed wool of various hues, are world-famous and in great demand. A large tapestry may take him as long as a year to finish. Vásquez proudly explained that the cochineal dyes are—unlike synthetic dyes—virtually permanent, because they resist fading from light and washing. To prove his point, he showed Ross a three-hundred-year-old red wool skirt that was almost as bright as newly dyed wool, even though, Ross notes, "it had been scrubbed and beaten on rocks with harsh detergents and exposed to the intense tropical sun immeasurable times."

According to Michael Kosztarab, three Old World insects were important sources of red dyes before the Spanish learned about cochineal from the Indians of the New World. The most widely used of them was a scale insect, kermes, that feeds on an evergreen oak that grows along the eastern Mediterranean coast and in more western parts of the Middle East. Phipson makes a fascinating etymological observation about the name *kermes:*

> The Kermes (*Coccus ilicis,* Latr.) has been employed to impart a scarlet colour to cloth from the earliest ages. It was known to the Phoenicians under the name of *Tola,* to the Greeks as *Kokkos,* and to the Arabians and Persians as Kermes or Alkermes (*Al* signifying *the,* as in the Arabian words alkali, alchymy, [algebra], etc.). In the Middle Ages it received the epithet *Vermiculatum,* or "little worm," from it having been supposed that the insect was produced from a worm. From these denominations have sprung the Latin *coccincus,* the French *cramoisi* and *vermeil,* and our *crimson* and *vermillion.*

(When I first met my prospective wife's family, they—confused about my career plans—asked me how I would ever make a living as an etymologist.)

The so-called Polish cochineal, also known as the "scarlet grain of Poland," is an unusual scale in that it feeds and lives on the roots of its host plant, *Knawel* in Polish, a member of the same family (Rubiaceae) as our North American bedstraw and the beautiful little bluets. Harvesting the scale was laborious work because the plants had first to be uprooted and then replanted. In 1864, Phipson noted that Polish cochineal had by then been largely replaced by the Mexican scale insect; "though still employed by the Turks and Armenians for dyeing wool, silk, and hair, but more particularly for staining the nails of the Turkish women, it is rarely used in Europe except by the Polish peasantry."

Another species of scale, the lac insect, has for centuries been famous as the source of shellac and as an ingredient in sealing wax (as you will see in chapter 5), but its secretions also yield a red dye, which is particularly successful on silk, explaining the early Chinese interest in it. Colonies of this insect live on the twigs of various trees in India and nearby countries. The females secrete a very thick layer of a hard, resinous substance, lac, that surrounds the twig and protects the colony. The dye is now seldom used and shellac has been largely replaced by synthetics.

The Aleppo gall, caused by a tiny wasp and found on oaks in eastern Europe and western Asia, forms a rich black dye when mixed with salts of iron. The immature galls, those from which the insect has not yet escaped, are—as Margaret Fagan points out—"of the most value and are the ones used in dyeing black." She writes:

> In the history of the art of dyeing, the Aleppo gall figures largely from the earliest mention of the art in literature up to the very present. According to Theophrastus it was used by the Greeks in dyeing wool and woolen goods and Pliny mentioned it as being used to stain the hair black and as the best adapted for the preparation of leather and the dyeing of skins. As the ancients could not conceive of a scholar's taking an active interest in the technical arts there is no record of how these galls were used, merely the statements that they were so used; and it was not until the end of the eighteenth century that any definite knowledge of these galls was sought.

The value of the Aleppo gall, also known as the Turkish gall, lies in its unusually high content of tannic acid—about 65 percent. It is the tannic acid that is the basis of the black dye and, as you will see in chapter 6, of the best inks for writing.

Following the invention of the first synthetic dye in 1856—soon followed by the synthesis of many others—the international market for cochineal and other natural dyes rapidly collapsed. By 1875, cochineal plantations had been abandoned and poverty and distress reigned in once-prosperous cochineal-producing areas. Chester Jones tells us that by 1883, Guatemala's cochineal exports had fallen from the 1858 high of a million pounds to only a little more than 18,000 pounds, and by 1884 to a mere 812 pounds. By 1887, the price of cochineal had fallen to a ruinous one-tenth of its maximum and barely covered the cost of production.

Nevertheless, the production of cochineal has continued, albeit on a much smaller scale. To this day, cochineal farming persists in Peru and the Canary Islands. It is the source of the dye known commercially as carmine red, which, according to Gabriel Lauro, a cofounder of La Monde, Ltd., the Natural Color Company, is now used mainly to color foods, beverages, and pharmaceuticals even though the dye is expensive and in rather short supply. Natural colors such as cochineal, Lauro explains, are preferred by manufacturers of these products because of a 1990 amendment to the Federal Food, Drug, and Cosmetic Act that requires nutritional labeling of foods, including the listing of colorants added to improve the appearance of the product. Some artificial dyes have been found to be carcinogenic. Consequently, consumers tend to be suspicious—sometimes rightly so—of artificial dyes added to foods. Lauro tells us that "rabbinical authorities have determined that cochineal is not Kosher." This is in keeping with the biblical proscription against eating insects and other creeping things except for grasshoppers, locusts, and related leaping insects such as crickets (Leviticus 11:20–33).

Insects play a part in the dyeing of cloth beyond being a source of dyes. The wax secreted by honey bees is used in an ancient process of dyeing cloth to produce patterns known as batik. A wax crayon, often made of beeswax, is used to draw a pattern on a piece of cloth. Then the cloth is dipped into a water-based dye of a color that contrasts with the original color of the cloth. While the greasy wax repels the dye, the dye soaks into the uncovered cloth. When the wax is removed with hot water, the pattern, in the original color of the cloth, contrasts with the color of the newly applied dye.

Insects not only supply us with the silk that is woven into cloth to cover our bodies and a dye to color the silk; since ancient times they or their products have also been used as ornaments of many different types. As we will see next, cocoons, insect galls, insect wings, whole dead insects, and even living insects have been, and are still, worn as decorations to embellish the human body and used as models for decorative items such as jewelry.

IV Baubles, Bracelets, and Anklets

Imagine my surprise when, on my way home from Mexico some years ago, I saw a large living beetle tethered by a thin silver chain crawling sluggishly on the jacket of a well-dressed middle-aged woman sitting near me on the airplane. It looked to me like a large relative of the famous Egyptian scarab (which you will meet in chapter 5). The use of living insects as jewelry, notes F. Tom Turpin in *Insect Appreciation,* is not at all uncommon. Large, hardy beetles that do not feed in the adult stage are "commonly collected in Mexico and with rhinestones and a delicate chain cemented to a wing cover, become... living brooch[es]." Tourists who buy living jewelry seldom get to show it off back home. A federal law prohibits importing live insects into the United States without a permit—and these permits are difficult to obtain even by professional entomologists for research purposes. Consequently, such live-beetle brooches are confiscated at border inspection stations. As the Bible tells us, "There is no new thing under the Sun" (Ecclesiastes 1:9): more than one hundred years ago in England, according to Paul Beckmann, Victorian ladies wore colorful, iridescent "jewel beetles" tethered to their clothing by tiny gold chains.

I know of only two other ways in which insects have served as living jewelry. In their *Introduction to Entomology,* first published in 1815, William Kirby and William Spence describe the use of light-flashing fireflies as ornaments: "In India, as I am informed by Major Moore and Captain Green, [the ladies] . . . have recourse to fire-flies, which they enclose in gauze and use as ornaments for their hair when they take their evening walks." In my mind's eye, I can picture beautiful women wearing elegant and flatteringly draped saris of red silk embroidered with gold thread walking along a tree-lined avenue with their shining black hair accented by glittering, flashing fireflies.

In his *Curious Facts in the History of Insects,* published in 1865, Frank Cowan notes that throughout the islands of the Caribbean "the *cucuju* [firefly] is worn by the ladies as a most fashionable ornament. As many as fifty or a hundred are sometimes worn on a single ballroom dress. Capt. Stuart tells me he once saw one of these insects upon a lady's white collar, which at a little distance rivaled the Kohinoor in splendor and beauty. The insect is fastened to the dress by a pin that pierces its body, and is worn only while it is still alive, for it no longer emits light after it dies." I hope that this cruelty has long been out of fashion.

Insects have, of course, long been and are still models for jewelry. In Beckmann's book, loaded with vivid color illustrations of strikingly beautiful beetles, you will learn that the scarab beetles, considered in the next chapter, "have been rendered in gold and precious stone, in enamel and glass by the major jewellery designers of the nineteenth and twentieth centuries. Louis C. Tiffany created scarabs of iridescent glass and many of Cartier's jewels incorporated antique Egyptian scarabs. The scarab exudes an irresistible charisma, even in the modern imagination, and scarab jewelry is still thought to bring luck to its wearer."

During the Victorian era, notes R. W. Wilkinson, the insect brooch was a popular genre of women's jewelry. He reports that a large collection of Victorian jewelry was auctioned by the Parke-Bernet Galleries in 1969, including several pieces of insect jewelry. Some of them were *en tremblant.* That is, their wings—attached by hidden coil springs—moved and seemed to flap with the slightest motion of the body. Twelve of the eighteen insect pieces were butterflies, two were beetles, two dragonflies, one a bee, and another, an insect relative, a spider. The popularity of insect jewelry during the Victorian era probably reflected the public's widespread and strong interest in insects and other "products of nature" in those days. It was an exciting time, when previously unknown plants, insects, and other creatures from faraway jungles, deserts, and savannas were every year discovered by the thousands, a time when Charles Darwin's books, and books by other naturalist-explorers such as Alfred Russel Wallace (codiscoverer of the theory of evolution) and Henry W. Bates, were best sellers. In those days, the American public flocked to the popular chautauquas and other venues to hear lectures by naturalists and geologists such as the then nationally famous Jean Louis Agassiz, a Swiss-born professor at Harvard University and the first to propose that there had been an ice age when glaciers covered much of Europe.

An acquaintance who is a jeweler told me that fashions in jewelry come and go. Insect jewelry will be in vogue for a time, then ebb in popularity, and eventually come back into fashion. By paging through upscale sales catalogues, Turpin got the impression that insect jewelry—particularly butterfly jewelry—is once again very popular. In my usual obsessive way, I felt compelled to actually count how often animals, particularly insects, were models for jewelry and other ornaments in the two most recent issues of the Smithsonian sales catalogue. Animals of one sort or another appeared 218 times: 61 birds, 67 furry mammals, and 36 other, not-so-cuddly four-legged

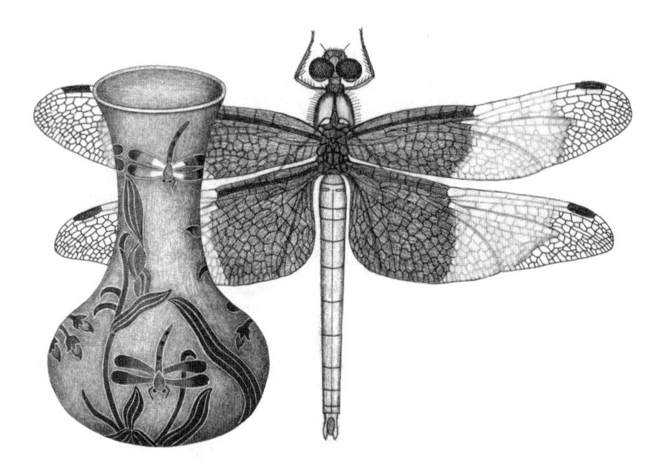

animals. Six-legged animals—that is, insects—were well represented with a total of 54, including 38 butterflies, 11 dragonflies, 3 ladybird beetles, 1 bee, and also 1 spider. I see quite a few women wearing insect jewelry. There are many butterflies, but dragonflies are surprisingly popular and are likely to be beautifully made and elegant. My dearest friend wears a large silver dragonfly pin with filigree wings and turquoise beads for eyes. An acquaintance wears a large dragonfly pin beautifully crafted of silver by a Navajo artisan, which also has turquoise eyes but has delicate wings carved of mammoth ivory.

If you are ever in Bogotá, Colombia, do not fail to visit the wonderful gold museum. In one large room there is a breathtakingly beautiful display of hundreds of pieces of gleaming jewelry and other objects superbly crafted

Above: A ceramic vase decorated with stylized dragonflies, one of which resembles the beautiful widow skimmer shown behind the vase.

of gold by pre-Columbian artisans. Such objects have been recovered from the bottom of a Colombian lake, where they were "sacrificed" during a ritual honoring an exalted ruler. We are lucky to have them. Almost all other golden artifacts, except for inaccessible grave goods, were melted down and shipped to Spain by the gold-hungry conquistadores.

What, you ask, do this pre-Columbian jewelry and other golden artifacts have to do with insects? The answer is that artisans of advanced New World cultures used beeswax in the casting of gold—not the wax of the Old World honey bee, but that of the New World stingless bees. (These two insects appear in later chapters.) The casting is made by the "lost wax" process. Herbert Schwarz quotes an English translation of an account of this process, as used by the Aztecs, written in Nahuatl (the language of the Aztecs) by Father Bernardo de Sahagún in the sixteenth century. For example, a small solid casting—such as a piece of jewelry—is made by encasing a solid beeswax replica of the jewel in clay. When the clay is fired in a kiln, the wax melts and is drained off (lost) through a small hole, and molten gold is poured into the resulting hollow form.

The Kofan Indians of western Colombia, notes D. C. Geijskes of the Museum of Natural History in Leiden, the Netherlands, incorporate insect or insect parts in necklaces, headbands, ear tassels, and nose plugs. Borys Malkin, a collector of insects and "Amerindian ethnographicas," sent Geijskes a photograph of a Kofan woman wearing as an adornment the front wing of a damselfly (a dragonfly relative) inserted into a feather shaft nose plug. The wing, close to 2 inches long, is marked with an intricate and beautiful netlike pattern of thin, dark veins and has a large vivid yellow spot at its very tip. At its inner margin the yellow spot is ringed by a dark brown area, which fades toward the base of the wing. Particularly attractive to the Kofans are the 2-inch-long wing covers of a giant metallic wood-boring beetle, which shine like smoothly polished copper. (Wing covers are hardened front wings, "armor plating," which cover most of a beetle's upper side.) Walter Linsenmaier's words apply to many species of this large family of beetles (Buprestidae), which includes the bronzed birch borer and the emerald ash borer, both destructive insects that have beautifully iridescent wing covers: "Like living jewels . . . they sun themselves on flowers, leaves, wood, and bark, scattering their magnificent hues everywhere."

Frank Cowan remarks on the eye-catching metallic sheen of these exceptionally attractive beetles:

> Many species of the *Buprestidae* are decorated with highly brilliant metallic tints, like polished gold upon an emerald ground, or azure upon a ground of gold; and their elytra, or wing-coverings, are employed by the ladies of China, and also of England, for the purpose of embroidering their dresses. The Chinese have also attempted imitations of these insects in bronze, in which they succeed so well that the copy may be sometimes mistaken for the reality. In Ceylon and throughout India, the golden wing-cases of two of this tribe . . . are used to enrich the embroidery of the Indian zenana [harem], while the lustrous joints of the legs are strung on silken threads, and form necklaces and bracelets of singular brilliancy.

At one time, notes Beckmann, the wing covers of beetles "were harvested by the millions in the hardwood forests of Burma for export to India," where they were sewn onto fabrics with metallic threads.

In the Bahamas and South Africa, A. D. Imms writes, ground pearls are collected from the soil around grass roots and strung to make necklaces. The "pearls" are actually dormant female scale insects (family Margarodidae) enclosed in spherical capsules of hard, lustrous wax that may be as much as a third of an inch in diameter. Scale insects, distant relatives of the aphids, are so called because many species, the armored scales (family Diaspididae), secrete a hard waxen scale that covers the body. For most of their lives the armored scales lack any appendages except for a sap-sucking beak that is permanently embedded in their host plant. They are essentially blob-like plant parasites. The ground pearls are among an exceptional group of scale insects, which includes the cochineal insect, that are not covered by a scale but generally secrete waxen filaments that cover the body when they are not dormant. Unlike the armored scales, the females have short, weak legs, but they are capable of only very limited movement.

The Aguaruna, a tribe of the Jivaroan language family of eastern Peru, may well be, according to a 1978 article by Brent Berlin and Ghillean Prance, unique in their use of insect galls as body ornamentation. A gall, a tumorlike swelling on a plant, is caused by and is the food of a larval insect that hatches from an egg inserted into the plant by its mother and that lives in a chamber in the gall. The galls in question, caused by an insect that had yet to be identified when Berlin and Prance published their article, develop on the underside of the leaves of a tree that the Aguaruna call *dúship.* This tree was then new to science. That is, it had not been scientifically described and given a scientific name. These galls are doughnut-shaped and about three-sixteenths of an inch in diameter. "When the tree sheds its leaves," note Berlin and Prance, "they are gathered in baskets by the Aguaruna who later remove the galls for use in necklaces. The [indented] center of the gall may... be closed by a thick membrane which is easily perforated by a sharp, pointed object." These natural beads are then strung to make necklaces. A person may wear as many as forty looped strands, each about 50 inches long. Since each strand includes more than a thousand galls, this person would be wearing well over forty thousand galls.

The Aguaruna think the galls are seeds, and the chieftain of another tribe believed them to be fruits. Berlin and Prance quote an account of a conversation with this chieftain, Tariri, sent to them by a missionary: "Tariri laughed when I said it [the gall] was derived from an insect egg. He said, 'It can't possibly be. It grows right along the veins of the leaves. Do you think we don't know a fruit when we see one?'"

H. F. Schwarz recounts how the Aborigines of northern Australia enhanced their coiffures by attaching balls or beads made of the wax of stingless bees "to the ends of wisps of their hair." They enhanced the decorative value of these ornaments by pressing small scarlet seeds into the wax. The Indians of southern Brazil—and no doubt of other South American areas—used the wax of stingless bees to attach decorative feathers to their finery.

In 1900, the eminent entomologist Leland Howard described head rings made of insect wax that are worn by the Zulus and "Kaffirs" of southern Africa: "This head-ring was early noticed by African explorers, and it was said to have been made of sinews surrounded with wax, massed on with the help of oil. The head is [partly] shaven, and some of the hair is worked up into the ring to hold it. As the hair grows, the ring is pushed up and must occasionally be reformed to some extent." The wax is said to be secreted by a scale insect of the genus *Ceroplastes* (from the Latin word for wax and the Greek word for molded). Howard says of this genus: "These . . . insects are extensive wax producers. The old Chinese wax of commerce, for example, is secreted by *Ceroplastes ceriferus.* The exact species of *Ceroplastes* from which the Zulus get their wax is, I believe, not known."

A mask made from the paper nest of a colony of bald-faced hornets is certainly one of the most unusual uses of an insect product. One of these football-shaped nests, according to Roger Akre and his coauthors, may be as much as 14 inches in diameter and 24 inches long and occupied by a colony consisting of one queen and numerous workers. Multilayered walls enclose a large space in which hang three to five tiers of horizontal paper combs with many hexagonal cells, in each of which the queen wasp lays a single egg that the workers raise to maturity on a diet of insects. The paper of which the nest is composed, Karl von Frisch tells us, is made of wood fibers that the worker wasps shave off dead wood—perhaps a fallen tree or a fence post—with their mandibles and bind together with saliva. Gerald McMaster and Clifford Trafzer report that the Cherokee of North Carolina wore masks in their traditional dances—masks made of wood in animal dances and usually of gourds for the booger dances intended to drive away evil spirits that cause sickness. But on at least one occasion, a booger dancer hastily made a mask by removing the combs from a wasp nest and making holes for the eyes and the mouth.

Ankle bracelets adorned with dry cocoons containing a few pebbles, seeds, or even fragments of ostrich eggshell produce a rustling sound as a shaman, stamping his feet, sings and dances over an ailing person during a curing ceremony. Such a ceremony, says Richard Peigler, might be seen in southern Africa or, on the other side of the Atlantic, in the western United States and northern Mexico. In either place, the cocoons will not be those of the mulberry silkworm, but are likely to be those of some species of the family Saturniidae, a giant silk moth, a relative of cecropia, cynthia, promethea, and the atlas moth. This is an exceptionally striking anthropological parallel. In this case, widely separated people of different cultures have independently developed similar or almost identical rattles.

Anklets may be of two styles. One is exemplified by the rattles of the natives of southern Africa. Howard notes that "the use of these ankle rattles has become quite general in Natal since the introduction of the rickshaw from China and India." The African rickshaw men "wear the anklets very generally, and their rattle on the streets is almost as familiar as sleigh-bells in a New England town in winter." Howard explains that

> the natives collect the cocoons after the moth has issued, put one or more small stones into each cocoon and sew them onto a broad strip of monkey skin, side by side, so as to cover the surface of the skin. They are sewn to the raw side of the hide, the fur being on the opposite side. The anklets ... are 10 inches long by 4 inches wide and are attached to the [ankles] by means of thongs.... The cocoons are tough and dry, and the stones within them rattle in a most delightful way.

The other style, used by several tribes in the New World and by the various San (Bushmen) tribes of the Kalahari Desert in southern Africa, consists of strands—each as much as 6 feet long—of dozens to a hundred or more cocoons strung or sewn onto lengths of cordage or cloth. These rattles are wound around the lower leg from the knee to the ankle. Anklets made by the San in Botswana are as much as 60 inches long and consist of as many as seventy-two cocoons. The cocoons are slit open along their original line of attachment to a twig, and gravel or bits of ostrich eggshell are placed in them. Natives in Natal, reported A. Schultze in 1913, made similar strands of cocoons that they wore as belts around the waist.

A similar anklet, still made and used by the Yaqui of Arizona and the Mexican state of Sonora, relates Peigler, consists of cocoons sewn onto red yarn. Red tassels on the two ends of the anklet "are called 'flowers' and symbolize divine grace." Arizona Yaqui paint their cocoons white to keep them looking new, because they have no local supply of cocoons to make new anklets, but must import them from Yaqui in Sonora. For some years even the Yaqui of Sonora had to obtain cocoons from a neighboring tribe because the moth population in their area was decimated by the Mexican government's massive sprayings of an herbicide to eradicate fields of marijuana.

Handheld rattles were used by various Indian tribes of California, Arizona, and Sonora. The "medicine rattle" most commonly used by the Pomo tribe was, according to Peigler, called *Kaiyōyō*, "after the oriole (*Kai yoyok*), a bird said to rattle when it talked." The rattle "had a stout wooden handle and had between 6 and 40 cocoons attached by large feather shafts, usually decorated with additional feathers." The Castanoan Indians made hand rattles from cocoons still fastened to the twig to which the spinning caterpillars had anchored them. Bound together with a strip of cloth, several of the twigs formed the handle of the rattle. Some observers thought that these Indians ate the pupae removed from the cocoons, but an anthropologist, Craig Bates, told Peigler that although they relished insects as food, the Indians probably did not eat pupae from cocoons that were to be made into rattles in deference to the "power" they associated with medicine rattles.

Shamans of the Miwok tribe believed that cocoon rattles were too powerful for "commoners" to handle. The supposed power of a rattle flowed from the ritual of its fabrication. Quartz pebbles or crystals were inserted into cocoons collected on the sunny side of a shrub on a mountain slope. Craig Bates quoted an observer who saw a Miwok shaman make a rattle: "Four cocoons . . . large and of a lustrous, natural, silvery color are tied to a stick . . . trimmed with eagle down and feathers from the side of an eagle. . . . [It] had a leather loop as a handle and four single strips of skin . . . from which hung two eagle feathers and two tiny white pigeon feathers. It was truly a work of art."

In response to a report that a smallpox epidemic might reach his village from a neighboring village, a shaman named Chiplichu performed a *hiweyi* dance. Accompanied by twelve other men, he danced from sunset to midnight on four successive nights. E. Breck Parkman quotes a witness who described the shaman's costume:

> Chiplichu wore a feather boa called *hichli,* which passed across the back of his neck and was drawn back under his arms from the front, the two ends being joined behind to form a tail. He carried a cocoon rattle, called *wasilni,* in each hand, and a third cocoon rattle was fastened in his hair. He wore a wreath on his head, made of stems and leaves of mugwort... twisted together.... Four bunches of split crow feathers attached to sticks completed his headdress. Each of these feather ornaments was about two feet long and tied with deer sinew. They were thrust in his hair, one sticking out in front, another in back, and one on each side. The cocoon rattle which he wore on his head was fastened at the back, with the rattles up. A tule [reed] mat, said to be six inches thick, with armholes, was worn very much like a skirt and reached to the knees.

Chiplichu asked a spirit if his village was truly threatened. It replied, "There is no sickness coming at all."

Various other peoples, Peigler reports, have found uses for the cocoons of giant silk moths. The Wailaki of California made a handheld charm by weaving tule on a cross of willow sticks, forming a diamond shape with its center where the sticks cross. One cocoon containing gravel from an anthill hung from each of three of the protruding ends of the sticks; the fourth end was the handle. Peigler suggests that "the purpose of these objects was to focus the eye of a god on the person holding it, ensuring health or success in a particular endeavor." A cocoon of a psychid moth, a bagworm not related to the giant silk moths, was one "of an assortment of fetishes in a gourd container used by a medicine man in Zaire." In Taiwan, Atlas moth cocoons were made into pocket purses for the tourist trade. They were about 2.4 inches long, equipped with a zipper, and were labeled "wallet made of wild silk" in Chinese.

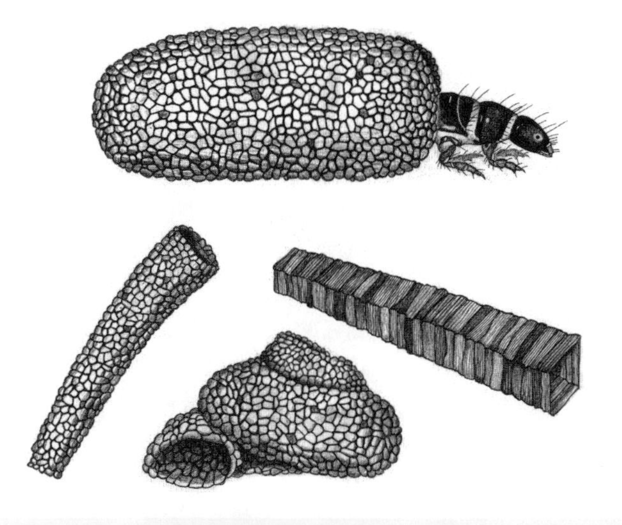

Making jewelry from the "cocoons" of caddisfly larvae (order Trichoptera), a craft that I had never heard of, was recently described in a Knight Ridder release that appeared in my local newspaper. But first, let me tell you a little about caddisflies, which are not really flies at all. The larvae are caterpillar-like and live in ponds and streams, and many are quite mobile. The adults, mothlike insects with somewhat hairy wings, are often seen flitting around lights at night near water. The larvae of many species make and live in portable, tubelike shelters, "cocoons" that cover all but their heads and legs, and that they wear much as a hermit crab wears its shell. Many construct their tubes, or cases, of grains of sand and small stones bound together with silk. A case may be a splendid mosaic of multicolored grains of sand as closely spaced as the tiles in a mosaic made by human hands.

Above: A caddisfly larva in its case (top), a tubelike and a snail-shaped case made of sand grains (lower left), and another made of plant fragments (lower right).

But Kathy Stout improves on nature. She raises caddisfly larvae in captivity and supplies them with unusual, to say the least, building materials—as the newspaper says, with "opals, garnets, tiger's eye, jasper, lapis, gold nuggets, emeralds, rubies, sapphires, and even diamonds." Ultimately, the larva pupates in its case, metamorphoses, and flies off as an adult. At that point, Kathy collects the empty cases—each an inch or more long, beautiful, and with no two alike—and fills them with epoxy to ensure that they stay together. Then her mother, Marilyn Kyle, uses the cases to design unique jewelry—everything from earrings to necklaces—"which sell for from $35 to $2,000." People love her jewelry. Kathy says, "Men like it because they can say, 'That was made by an insect. That's cool.'"

It seems that there is really no new thing under the sun. While paging through Henry McCook's *Tenants of an Old Farm,* a quaint and delightful ramble through nature published in 1886, I came upon his method for forcing a caterpillar of the clothes moth (*Tinea pellionella*) to make a multicolored tubular case—in which it lives much as a caddisfly larva lives in its case. The caterpillar, which feeds on woolens in our closets and chests, festoons its silken case with bits of lint from the cloth on which it feeds. As the caterpillar grows, it lengthens its case. McCook writes: "By shifting the caterpillar from one colored cloth to another the required tints are produced, and the pattern is gained by watching the creature at work, and transferring it at the proper time. For example, a half-grown caterpillar may be placed upon a piece of bright green cloth. After it has made its tube, it may be shifted to a black cloth" and then transferred to a piece of scarlet cloth. "In this way the little worm, by friendly human manipulations, may by-and-by find itself arrayed, like the favorite son of Jacob, in a 'coat of many colors.'"

We have seen that insects or insect products have been used by people to clothe or otherwise adorn themselves. We next consider some other insect products that are not as attention-grabbing but nevertheless are or have been very important to people: candles made of beeswax; shellac made from lac, the secretion of certain scale insects; and sealing wax composed of a mixture of beeswax and lac.

V Candles, Shellac, and Sealing Wax

In 1569, Father João dos Santos, a Portuguese missionary to the Sofala tribe in what is now Mozambique, wrote that from time to time a small bird would fly through the windows of his mission church and eat bits of wax from the candlesticks on the altar. Herbert Friedmann, who quotes the priest, goes on to say that the priest referred to the bird as *sazu passaro que come cera,* "sazu [its native name], a bird that eats wax." Later I will come back to the fascinating behavior of this little bird, but first I need to tell you that the candles in the mission chapel were formed from beeswax that was made by the very same species of honey bee that produces the honey that you put on your toast, the western honey bee (*Apis mellifera*), native to western Eurasia and Africa and long ago established in the New World by Europeans.

The bees use wax to construct the combs of hexagonal cells in which they raise larvae and store pollen and nectar. When the colony is expanding and needs more cells, some of the stay-at-home workers ("house bees")—too young to leave the nest to forage for pollen and nectar—secrete scales of wax from eight glands on the underside of the abdomen. They first gorge on honey, and then, after a day of rest, they will have converted the sugar in the honey to wax, which is a lipid, a fat. This conversion is familiar to all of us. After all, if we eat sweets in excess, we put on unwanted layers of fat. In his captivating and eminently readable *On the Hive and the Honey-Bee,* first published in 1853, Lorenzo Langstroth reported: "The most careful experiments have clearly established the fact that at least twenty pounds of honey are consumed in making a single pound of wax. If any think that this is incredible, let them bear in mind that wax is an animal oil secreted from honey, and let them consider how many pounds of corn or hay they must feed to their stock in order to have them gain a single pound of fat."

Over the millennia, people have found a multitude of uses for beeswax, which is still a valuable commodity. According to my colleague Gene Robinson, its worth per pound is two to three times as great as that of honey. The earliest uses of beeswax are lost in prehistory. But as we learn from Holley Bishop's fascinating and informative book on bees, beeswax—available in the markets of ancient Egypt, Greece, Mesopotamia, and Rome—had many uses in the ancient world. The Egyptians, for example, made mummies of their embalmed dead by wrapping their bodies in multiple layers of linen cloth that had been soaked with molten beeswax. The mummies were then placed in coffins sealed with beeswax. In ancient Greece, molten beeswax mixed with a pigment was painted on walls to create a lustrous finish. In a similar way, boats were waterproofed with a coat of beeswax that was often pigmented; and from Mesopotamia to China, artists used beeswax in the "lost wax" method of casting figurines and other objects, which I described in chapter 4.

About one hundred years ago, Roger Morse relates, "a woman's sewing kit would not have been complete without a piece of . . . beeswax, usually a lump about half the size of a hen's egg." The wax was used to weld together the loose ends of thread or to make a needle more slippery. Beeswax was once used by dentists to take impressions of patients' teeth, and, as I learned from Anturco Dental Laboratories in Champaign, Illinois, it remains a component of the waxes used in fashioning dentures and casting gold crowns. It is still, according to my pharmacist, used in preparing ointments and skin creams. Beeswax has been a component of furniture polish, shoe polish, munitions, electrical insulators, and many other products. But for some uses, beeswax has been replaced by less expensive synthetic resins and waxes such as paraffin.

The beekeepers themselves are among the best customers for beeswax—in the form of comb foundation. The foundation is a thin sheet of beeswax with the bases and the beginnings of the walls of the hexagonal cells, of just exactly the size preferred by the bees, embossed on both sides by a stamping process. Foundations are mounted in a rectangular wooden frame and installed in the hive. The bees, ever practical and opportunistic, reduce their need for wax by completing the embossed pattern to finish the comb. Since the first foundation was stamped by hand with a wooden press in 1857, its manufacture has been mechanized, and by the end of the nineteenth century inexpensive foundation was readily available. Today, virtually all American beekeepers use mass-produced foundation.

In *Insects and Human Society,* T. Michael Peters quotes an English beekeeper who, in 1827, wrote that beeswax "is become the greatest supply of light in all polite assemblies, as well as in the Romish churches, in which wax-candles are kept constantly burning. By this means, wax is become a considerable article of commerce, and as such, is now become the chief inducement for the care bestowed on bees, especially in the warmer climates."

Morse suggests that making candles to be used in churches, a practice that dates back to antiquity in the Roman Catholic Church, is today probably the principal use of beeswax. "It is especially suitable for candles because it burns with less smoke and odor than do animal fats and tallows; in fact burning beeswax has a rather pleasant odor." Furthermore, the honey bee has symbolic significance in the Roman Catholic Church: "Certain church liturgy suggests that, since the honey bee [worker] is a virgin, the wax produced by her is symbolic of purity." A telephone call to M. Andrew Heckman, the director of St. John's Catholic Chapel at the University of Illinois in Champaign, revealed that the chapel still uses candles made largely of beeswax, but not of pure beeswax as in previous centuries. Most of the candles burned in the chapel consist of 51 percent beeswax and the rest paraffin, a synthetic petroleum derivative, but others, used for special purposes, are 67 percent beeswax.

In the sixteenth century, the conquering Spaniards converted the Indians of Mexico, Central America, and South America to Catholicism, often by force. One of the conquistadores who helped Hernán Cortés subjugate these native peoples was Bernal Díaz del Castillo. As related by Herbert Schwarz, Díaz recounted that the Spaniards erected an altar at which mass was celebrated by the padre Fray Bartolomé de Olmedo and that they showed the Indians the way to "make candles of the native wax and ordered these candles always to be kept burning on the altar." This native wax was produced, not by our familiar honey bee, but by the tropical New World stingless bees you will become acquainted with in chapter 8. The Indians valued this wax—it was among the many items sold at the great market at Tenochtitlán—and had long used it for purposes other than making candles. The Aztecs had a name for it: *xico-cuitlatl,* bee resin.

In the Maya village of Chan Kom, Schwarz tells us, wax from stingless bees was still used for making ceremonial candles until at least the late 1940s. The candle makers hang about fifty wicks from a horizontal wooden ring, and "as this ring is revolved, melted wax is poured over the wicks until the desired diameter [of candle] is attained." Because some hives produce wax of a darker color than others, the candles may be yellow or black. "Candles of black wax are occasionally lighted at funerals of adults and at that part of the All Soul's Day ceremonies when there is commemoration of the adult dead." Black candles are considered very sacred by the Maya of Honduras. A Mayan refused to sell black candles or exchange them for white ones because he believed that "white candles were devoid of a soul."

Honey bees, as Charles Michener enthusiastically informs us, are marvelous insects. They have what is probably the most complex social organization of any animal other than our own species. A colony, housed in a commercial hive or possibly in a hollow tree or a space in the walls of a building, includes just one queen, who is essentially an egg-laying machine, and thousands of workers, all sterile females. The older workers collect pollen and nectar, the food on which the younger workers raise larvae, almost all of which will mature to become workers except for a few drones (males) and, under special circumstances, a queen. Once every two or three years, a colony divides into two parts. The old queen and a large swarm of workers leave the old colony to found a new colony elsewhere. Unless a beekeeper captures the swarm and installs it in a hive box, it will become a feral colony and set up housekeeping elsewhere, perhaps in a hollow tree. The new queen and a large contingent of workers remain behind. The new queen will have returned to the nest from several afternoon mating flights to some site that is attractive to the drones, where they—even the first time they leave the hive—congregate in large numbers. The queen, who will never mate again, has an organ, the spermatheca, in which she will store as many as seven million live sperm—contributed by several drones—for as long as she lives, which may be several years.

The survival of a colony depends on the workers' extraordinary capabilities, two of which I find especially interesting: their dance language, which we will consider in chapter 8, and the way in which they heat and air-condition their nests. A colony of honey bees survives the cold of winter by creating heat. The workers crowd together, forming a tight cluster surrounding the queen and some honey-filled combs. The bees at the periphery of the cluster form an insulating layer, a "blanket" two bees thick, by crowding together "shoulder to shoulder." The inner bees, less tightly packed, keep the cluster warm by eating honey and converting its calories to heat by "shivering" their wing muscles without moving their wings. The workers constantly change positions to relieve those at the periphery.

In Japan, another species of honey bee (*Apis cerana*) uses its heat-producing ability to kill giant hornets that enter their nests to prey on the larvae. If a hornet scout enters the nest, according to Masato Ono and his coauthors, five hundred or more bees quickly surround it, forming a tight ball. Then they raise the temperature within that ball to an amazing 116°F, which is lethal to the hornet but not to the bees.

In summer, the workers use progressively more effective methods to cool the nest as its air temperature climbs above the optimum 95°F. If only a little cooling is required, they just fan their wings to circulate the air. The next step up is evaporative cooling, done by spreading a thin film of water on the combs. If that's not enough, the workers increase the rate of evaporation by vigorously fanning their wings. These measures are very effective. When Martin Lindauer placed a hive on a field of black lava rock where the air temperature was 158°F at the level of the hive, the workers kept the temperature in the hive at 95°F as long as there was a sufficient source of water nearby.

Let's now go back to the little bird that foraged for beeswax in that mission chapel in east Africa. Birds of this species do not ordinarily make a living by scrounging for candle drippings. They eat wax, bees, larvae, and honey from wild colonies. But the means by which they gain access to a colony of honey bees is very unusual indeed. When one of these birds locates a colony of wild bees, it finds a person—or an animal known as a honey badger—and, as Friedmann describes it, with rattling calls and a display of flapping wings and fanned tail feathers, leads the person (or honey badger) to the honey bee nest, which is likely to be in a hollow tree. From time to time, the bird pauses on a perch and displays vigorously to make sure that the person is following. After the person has torn open the nest and absconded with the combs of delicious honey, the bird—known as the honey guide (*Indicator indicator*)—moves in and makes a meal of the leftovers.

The honey guide is among the very few animals that can utilize wax as food. Most animals, including humans, cannot digest wax. The comb honey that we spread on our toast, still enveloped in wax, is considered a delicacy; we do, of course, digest the honey, but the wax just passes through us undigested. A few insects are among the animals that can utilize wax as a food. The one that beekeepers consider a threat to their hives is the greater wax moth (*Galleria melonella*). The female wax moth, explains Morse, "usually lays her eggs on the outside of the hive. The newly hatched, wax-eating larvae crawl into the hive and make silk-lined galleries in the honey comb, thus destroying it." The bees kill the wax moth caterpillars when they find them, but some wax moth caterpillars survive in out-of-the-way places where the bees seldom go, especially in weak colonies with a low population of workers. "When full grown," writes John Henry Comstock of the wax moth, "the larva is about 25 mm [1 inch] in length. It lies hidden in its gallery during the day, and feeds only at night, when the tired-out bees are sleeping the sleep of the just." In chapter 8 we will come back to the human taste for honey—said to be the food of the gods—which has been a welcome addition to the human diet at least as far back as the Stone Age.

Honey bees are by no means the only insects that secrete wax. Their close relatives the bumblebees, which are also social, form honeypots of wax in their nests, which are often located in abandoned mouse burrows in the ground. Quite a few other insects secrete wax. Most notable among them are the sap-sucking scale insects, relatives of the aphids, leafhoppers, and spittle insects. Most, if not all, of the scale insects are wax secretors. Among them are the ground pearls that you met in chapter 4. As you saw, the "pearls" are actually dormant female scale insects enclosed in a spherical capsule of hard wax. The armored scales, such as the tiny oyster shell scales that may infest your lilac bush, form a scalelike external armor of wax that protects the upper side of the body like a shield. (The oyster shell scale is so named because its scale looks like a tiny oyster shell.) Other scale insects, which do not actually form scales, may cover their bodies with an external coating of powdery wax or a dense covering of rather long waxy filaments. As pointed out by Douglas Miller and Michael Kosztarab, the females of some species, such as cottony cushion scales, also cover their egg masses with filaments of wax.

The wax made by scale insects, although neither as readily available nor as widely used as beeswax, has been employed for various purposes in many parts of the world. For example, the hard wax secreted by a close relative of the ground pearl, reports Katherine Jenkins, "has been exploited (sometimes cultivated) ... by peoples of Meso-America since before the Spanish Conquest." This wax forms a "tough impermeable film on any surface to which it is applied." Among its many uses are the waterproofing of wood and gourds, "binding pigments to surfaces in a lacquer-like coating, and as a base for face- and body-paint." In California, the native Indians, notes E. O. Essig, used resins and wax from the exudations of scale insects "for mending pottery, waterproofing baskets, fastening the sinew backing of bows, and even for chewing."

According to Michael Kosztarab, the Chinese wax scale (*Ericerus pela*) was probably the most important of the wax-making scale insects, producing large quantities of a pure white wax of which the Chinese made candles before paraffin became available. "In autumn," observes Frank Cowan, "the natives scrape this substance, which they call *Pela,* from off the trees, melt, purify, and form it into cakes. It is white and glossy in appearance, and, when mixed with oil, is used to make candles, and is said to be superior to the common wax [beeswax?] for use.... On the large cheeselike cakes of this wax, hanging in the grocers' and tallow-chandlers' shops at Hankow, there is often the written inscription: 'It mocks at the frost, and rivals the snow.'"

Actually, all insects—bedbugs, butterflies, beetles, and all the others—are protected by an exceedingly thin layer of wax that is not external but is, rather, a part of the insects' "skin." This skin, usually hard and armorlike, is known to entomologists as the body wall or cuticle and consists of three distinct layers. One of the microscopically thin outer layers, the epicuticle, includes an exceedingly thin layer of wax that helps to minimize the loss of water from the insect's body, a very important function because a drink of water is not generally available to most insects. The wax layer is covered and protected by a very thin covering of "cement." In 1945, Vincent Wigglesworth dramatically demonstrated the effect of removing a part of the wax layer from large blood-sucking bugs that normally drag their abdomens on the ground as they crawl. After they crawled over a surface sprinkled with an abrasive dust, much of the wax layer was worn away, and the bugs soon died from desiccation. But the cuticle of bugs whose abdomens were raised above the same surface by a peg of wax as they crawled was not abraded and they did not die, indicating that the dust did not act in some way other than by abrading away the wax layer.

Tucked away in a drawer in my living room is a 78 rpm phonograph record of Al Jolson and Bing Crosby singing duets. On one side of the disk is "Alexander's Ragtime Band" and on the other is "The Spaniard That Blighted My Life." The music is wonderfully toe-tapping, but what on earth, you ask, do Al Jolson and Bing Crosby have to do with insect products useful to people? These great singers are, of course, totally irrelevant to the subject. But the record itself is made from the secretions of certain scale insects. These tiny creatures secrete a resin known as lac. Lac has had many uses. At one time, before World War II, much of the world production of lac—mixed with fine clay, mica, or some other filler—was used to manufacture phonograph records. "In 1927–28," writes May Berenbaum, "Great Britain, Germany, and France collectively produced 260 million records, representing 18,000 tons of shellac." Beginning in the 1930s, however, the record industry gradually replaced shellac with synthetic plastics such as vinyl.

The lac insect, which has the apt scientific name *Laccifer lacca,* lives on fig, banyan, and various other trees in India, China, Sri Lanka, Taiwan, Vietnam, and the Philippines. Thousands of the minute newly hatched crawlers, explains F. C. Bishopp, settle down side by side on a twig or a young branch and insert their beaks into the plant tissue, and as they feed on sap and grow, they secrete a hard protective material, lac, which consists primarily of resin, wax, and coloring matter. This resinous secretion builds up around the insects, covers them, and completely encases the twig to a thickness of as much as a half inch and for a length of 4 to 5 inches. In about three

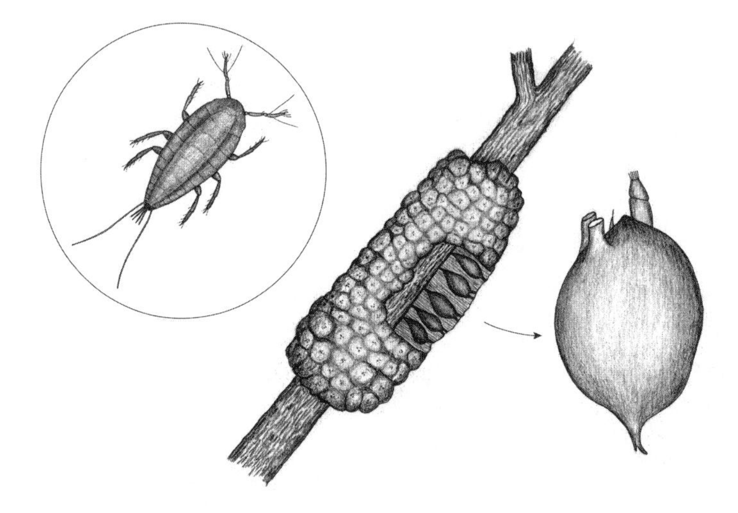

months, the insects mature. The sex ratio is greatly skewed; most of the crawlers develop into females, "which occupy small cavities in the resinous mass and from which they never emerge. The males do emerge and fertilize the females through the small openings which extend from their cavities to the surface of the encrustation. As the eggs develop in the body of the female, she assumes a saclike, bright-red appearance. . . . The females die, the eggs hatch, the crawlers escape and move to a nearby uninfested part of the twig, and the process is repeated."

In 1924, Elizabeth Brownell Crandall described the age-old, primitive way used in India to process lac. Jungle tribes collect the encrusted twigs and sell them. This stick lac is ground by hand in mortars and then sieved. "The crushed matter is divided into three parts: first, the wood, which is

---

Above: Stick lac. A colony of lac insects on a twig; a newly hatched nymph, a crawler, is on the left and an adult female is on the right.

used as fuel; second, the dust, 'khad,' sold to makers of bangles and toys; third, the true granular lac, which is known as Seed Lac." After the seed lac has soaked in water in stone troughs for twenty-four hours, a person steps into the trough and treads on the seed lac with bare feet, breaking it up into finer granules. The water becomes deep claret, and the granules are rinsed until all the color is removed. The seed lac is then spread out in the sun to dry.

> [It] is then put into long, narrow cloth bags, ten to twelve feet long and two inches wide.... These wormlike bags are held over open charcoal fires by two operators who begin to twist the bags in opposite directions, while the melted Lac slowly oozes out and drops upon the floor.
>
> During the process of melting, the foreman wields ... at intervals three implements—a long iron-hooded poker for stirring the fire, a wooden spoon for sprinkling water on the floor in front of the fire, and an iron scraper with which he scrapes the melted Lac from the outside of the bag. As the melted Lac drops to the floor, it is spread out by means of a pineapple leaf. Before it has time to congeal it is picked up by still another native, who stretches it into thin sheets, placing a foot on either end of the piece and then pulling it upward by means of his teeth and hands.

Each sheet is dried, broken up into flakes, "and packed in bags or cases ready for shipment, when it then becomes what is known in commerce as Shellac." When Crandall wrote, this primitive process was beginning to be replaced by machines. Machine-processed lac is considered inferior to the T.N. (truly native) grade, however.

The claret coloring matter rinsed from lac was made into a dye that, Cowan reports, was "manufactured at Calcutta and sent to England.... [I]n 1806, and the two following years, the sales of it at India House equaled in point of coloring matter half a million of pounds' weight of Cochineal." He goes on to say that the East India Company saved a great deal of money "in the purchase of scarlet cloths dyed with this color and Cochineal conjointly, and without any inferiority in the color obtained." Although cochineal is, as you know, still used in small quantities, lac dye is no longer on the market.

Lac has had many uses for at least several thousand years, according to Robert L. Metcalf and Robert A. Metcalf. It was made into beads, buttons, and, mixed with fine sand, abrasives. Dissolved in alcohol, it became a varnish that was commonly referred to as shellac. Shellac was once important in finishing fine furniture and other wood products. But it has been largely replaced by the synthetic polyurethane, in part because a shellac finish becomes white and opaque if water is spilled on it, whereas a polyurethane finish does not.

The story of seals and sealing wax involves three insects: the honey bee, the lac insect, and—probably to your surprise—a dung beetle, the sacred scarab beetle of ancient Egypt. We will come back to this beetle after considering the uses of sealing wax and how it is applied. The sealing wax, usually in the form of a stick, is held over the document to be sealed; the tip of the stick is melted with a flame; and the molten drop that falls onto the document is impressed with an engraved die, or embosser, usually called the seal. In medieval and more recent times, seals were generally made of bronze, silver, or some other metal. In ancient times, they were also likely to be made of metal, but in Egypt and Assyria they were often made of stone or hard-baked clay. The seal of any of these materials is engraved with a signature or a distinctive design, perhaps a coat of arms, that is incised below the seal's surface, so that when the seal is impressed on the molten wax, it produces the design in relief, embossing it so that it projects above the surrounding surface. In ancient Egypt, the seal was often engraved on the bezel (face) of a ring. Such signet rings or seal rings were also very important in Europe in the Middle Ages. For example, an enormous ring of gilded bronze bearing the image of St. Peter fishing was and still is used by the pope as an official seal for pontifical documents.

Seals of these types were once widely used to authenticate documents, to indicate ownership, to make the flap of an envelope tamperproof, and, before the invention of the envelope, to close a folded letter to guarantee secrecy. Today, sealing wax is seldom used, but it is still around. Recently, an office supply store told me that they don't have it but could order it and get it to me in a couple of weeks. Later that day, I found boxes of white, silver, and gold sealing wax made in China among the bridal supplies in an arts and crafts store. Each stick has a wick that can be lit to melt the wax. Embossed with the bride's initial, the drop of hardened wax decorates and seals the envelopes containing the wedding invitations. The store sells seals—also made in China—engraved with all the letters of the alphabet.

In medieval Europe, sealing wax was composed of a mixture of beeswax and a substance known as Venice turpentine. This is not the liquid we now know as turpentine, but rather the thick, viscous resin of a conifer such as a pine or a terebinth, the latter a small tree related to the sumacs. (The word *turpentine* is derived from the name of this tree.) Beginning in the sixteenth century, when lac from Asia first became known in Europe, it was substituted for the beeswax and Venice turpentine mixture. In either case, the sealing wax was usually colored, sometimes with green and sometimes with vermilion, which was likely to have been derived from the cochineal insect.

According to Harry Weis, small effigies of the sacred scarab (*Scarabaeus sacer*) abound in archaeological sites in Egypt. As we will see later, this dung beetle was an important religious symbol for the ancient Egyptians, but it also served as a seal. According to Percy Newberry's *Ancient Egyptian Scarabs,* first published in 1905, scarab effigies, usually about three-quarters of an inch long, a half inch broad, and a quarter of an inch high, were occasionally made of gold or ivory, sometimes of baked clay, but most often of carved stone, such as the soft and easily worked steatite (soapstone) or even of hard stone such as green basalt, granite, lapis lazuli, amethyst, jasper, or agate. The convex upper side of the effigy is a stylized depiction of a scarab, and the flat underside is usually incised with hieroglyphics, often the name of the owner.

Early in Egypt's Greco-Roman period (323 B.C.E. to 30 C.E.), scarab effigies were still available and, as told to me by Douglas Brewer, director of the University of Illinois's Spurlock Museum in Urbana, were probably used with sealing wax introduced by the Romans. But long before that the underside of the scarab effigy was used to emboss a soft clay seal. According to Weis, this practice was very common, as indicated "by the very large number of bits of embossed clay that had been used to seal boxes, vases, and bags found in ancient ruins." A jar of honey, for example, might be protected from pilferers by wrapping its stopper and neck with a layer of clay embossed with the owner's seal. The contents of a cloth bag could be protected by embedding the two ends of the cord that ties its neck shut in an embossed lump of clay. The message written on a scroll of papyrus bound with a string could be protected from prying eyes in a similar way.

The sacred scarab, like many dung beetles, forms a large spherical ball of dung that may be larger than its body, rolls it across the ground to a suitable site, digs a hole, puts in the dung ball, lays an egg on it, and fills the hole with soil. The larva that hatches from the egg eats the dung and when it is full-grown molts to the pupal stage; after it sheds the pupal skin, the adult beetle digs its way out of the soil. The ancient Egyptians, Weis tells us, believed that the god Khepera caused the sun to move across the sky in the same way that the scarab rolls its ball across the sand. The Egyptian name of this scarab was *Kheper,* and the god Khepera was sometimes represented as a man with a scarab on or in place of his head. The beetle also represented the soul emerging from the mummy, just as the young adult beetle emerges from the ground and flies off, as the Egyptians thought, toward the sun and heaven. Hence, this insect was looked on as a symbol of regeneration and immortality.

In the next chapter we will see that insects have had and, to some extent, still have an important role in our ability to communicate by writing. We will find out how wasps make paper, and that the Chinese, the first to make paper, probably learned how to do it by watching wasps. We will also learn how wasps make galls and how certain galls from oak trees are used in the making of ink.

VI Paper and Ink

Noah's descendants all spoke the same language until they started building the tower of Babel to reach heaven. Then their arrogance so incensed God, Genesis tells us, that he scattered them over the Earth and "confounded their language" so that they could no longer understand one another. According to the science writer Andrew Lawler, there are indeed almost seven thousand different languages. (But Jessica Ebert reports that at least half of them will disappear in the next hundred years.) Fewer than one hundred scripts—ways of recording words on paper—have appeared over the millennia, however. For example, the alphabet the ancient Romans used to write Latin has persisted for well over two thousand years and now spells out the words of such disparate languages as Italian, Spanish, Portuguese, French, Catalan, English, German, Swedish, Icelandic, and even Turkish. Scripts tend to live on despite alien invasions, religious upheavals, changing languages, and the adoption of new languages. Lawler quotes the anthropologist Stephen Houston of Brigham Young University: "There is so much intense emotion invested in scripts, they tend to live longer than they have any right to."

Insects have been used, notes Charles Hogue, as symbols in some writing systems: "Insect forms were converted into hieroglyphs and pictograms in ancient Egyptian, . . . Mayan, and Chinese writing." In tombs of the Yin dynasty of China (sixteenth to eleventh century B.C.E.), according to J.H. Tsai, "the tortoise shells used as paper were found inscribed with the ideograms denoting the characters silk, silkworm, and mulberry tree." Also found were tortoise shells bearing ideograms for a species of honey bee and for the locust. Edward O. Wilson, the famed conservationist and authority on ants, writes: "In Japanese the word 'ant' is intricately written by linking two characters: one meaning 'insect,' the other meaning 'loyalty.'" This is in recognition of how closely bound and "loyal" these social insects are to one another. In each case, stylized symbols evolved from more or less realistic representations of the insect. The written language of the ancient Egyptians, according to Hogue, included hieroglyphs representing the scarab, the bee, and the grasshopper. A hieroglyph could stand for either a word or a phonetic sound—the latter in a way much like an English rebus. For example, in English a picture of a bee might be followed by a picture of a leaf to represent the word *belief.*

Various technologies for recording languages in written form have been devised. More than fifty-five hundred years ago, the Sumerians in what is now Iraq used reed styluses to impress wedge-shaped (cuneiform) symbols into soft, moist clay tablets that were later baked in a kiln. Beginning about five thousand years ago, Egyptian hieroglyphs were written with a reed brush and ink made from soot on paperlike sheets of papyrus, which consisted of pieces of the stems of papyrus reeds flattened and pressed together. (The name of this reed, notes Robert Claiborne, is the source of the word *paper.*) The ancient Germanic people, beginning nearly two thousand years ago, carved their runes on thin slabs of beech wood that were sometimes laced together with thongs to form what was known as a *Buch,* which is the German word for both beech and book, both of which came to the English language from the German root word.

About twenty-six hundred years before the present, the Maya of the Yucatán and Central America inscribed their hieroglyphs on a writing surface much like paper. Their books, known as codices, consisted, according to Charles Gallenkamp, of a single long strip of "paper" made of pounded vegetable fiber bound together by a natural gum and coated on both sides with white lime. After being inscribed with complex hieroglyphic characters, using vegetable and mineral paints, the manuscript was folded and enclosed between wooden or leather covers. The wanton destruction of a library of Mayan codices by the Spanish in the mid-sixteenth century, Gallenkamp points out, robbed future scholars of a treasury of information. He notes ironically that "the spirit of the Inquisition burned brightly" in a Franciscan monk, Diego de Landa. Enraged by the stubborn refusal of the Maya to abandon their religion, he ordered that the "pagan" codices in the library in the town of Mani be publicly burned in the town plaza.

The silken walls of a tent, a communal nest, constructed by one hundred or more cooperating Mexican butterfly caterpillars (*Eucheira socialis*) have served as a unique writing surface in both prehistoric and historic times. *Eucheira* is one of an extremely small number of gregarious nest-building butterflies, but there are many such gregarious species among the closely related moths. Just as silkworms are host-specific and will feed only on mulberry leaves, *Eucheira* caterpillars, report Peter Kevan and Robert Bye, will feed only on the leaves of madrone trees (species of *Arbutus*). "The Aztecs," notes Richard Peigler, "called [this] insect xiquipilchiuhpapálotla, which means butterfly that makes a pouch." He described the walls of the tent as resembling parchment paper in texture and color, and as being so tightly woven and tough that they could be cut only with a sharp knife. These silken sheets were being used as writing paper in Mexico at the time of the Spanish conquest. Frank Cowan writes, "The silk of the nests of [this] social caterpillar . . . was an object of commerce in the time of Montecusuma [*sic*]; and the ancient Mexicans pasted together the interior layers, which may be written upon without preparation, to form a white, glossy pasteboard."

True paper was being made by the Chinese in 200 B.C.E. or perhaps even earlier. This craft spread westward slowly. Until medieval times, European scribes penned manuscripts on parchment, a writing surface prepared from the skin of a sheep or a goat. But by the fourteenth century C.E., paper was well known in Europe, there were paper mills in several European countries, and paper was rapidly replacing parchment. Originally, paper was made by hand from fibers of crushed wood or other vegetable pulps that were suspended in water and caught on a fine wire screen to form a thin sheet of fiber that was pressed and compacted to flatten it and remove most of the water before it was air dried. Although paper making has become highly mechanized, this basic process has remained essentially unchanged. When documents and books were copied and recopied by hand, relatively little paper was made and used. But after Johannes Gutenberg independently invented movable type in about 1450 C.E. (it had previously been invented in China in the eleventh century C.E.), books became inexpensive and readily available, and the demand for paper soared. In 1993, for example, the value of paper manufactured in the United States alone was $129 billion.

There are two theories to explain how the Chinese learned to make paper. One is that women collected lint after washing clothes and formed and dried it to make sheets of paper. The other theory, which I favor for an obvious reason, is that the discovery was made by watching hornets or other colonial paper-making wasps masticate wood fibers into a pulp that they mixed with their saliva to make the paper of which their nests are composed.

One of the most familiar of these paper nests is that of the black-and-white bald-faced hornet (*Dolichovespula maculata*), which we met in chapter 4. You may have seen one of these grayish, football-shaped nests, as much as 14 inches in diameter and 24 inches long, hanging from the branch of a tree or shrub. The abandoned nests are conspicuous in winter after the leaves have fallen. As we have seen, the nest consists of a multilayered paper envelope that encloses a large space in which hang several tiers of horizontal paper combs, each with many hexagonal cells. In each of these cells the queen wasp lays a single egg. The larvae that hatch from the eggs are raised by the sterile workers on a diet of insects and in summer will grow to become yet more sterile workers. In autumn, the colony produces a large number of fertile queens and the first and only males of the year. The workers soon die. The males die after they have mated with one or more queens, but the queens survive the winter in a sheltered place such as a crevice in a cliff or a hollow tree. In spring they found new colonies, build a small starter nest, and raise the first small brood of workers by themselves.

When building the nest, the workers—or the queen, but only before she has raised her first brood of workers—collect fibers from the sound but weathered wood of dead trees or fences, from decayed wood, and from non-woody plants. J. Philip Spradbery explains that when a worker wasp has collected sufficient pulp, often a ball the size of her head, she (all workers are sterile females) flies off to the nest with the ball of pulp held in her mandibles. When she arrives at the nest, in this case on the outer envelope, the wasp thoroughly masticates the pulp and mixes it with saliva. She then attaches it to the edge of the envelope as a narrow strip by clamping it on with her mandibles as she moves backward. After the wasp has used up all of her

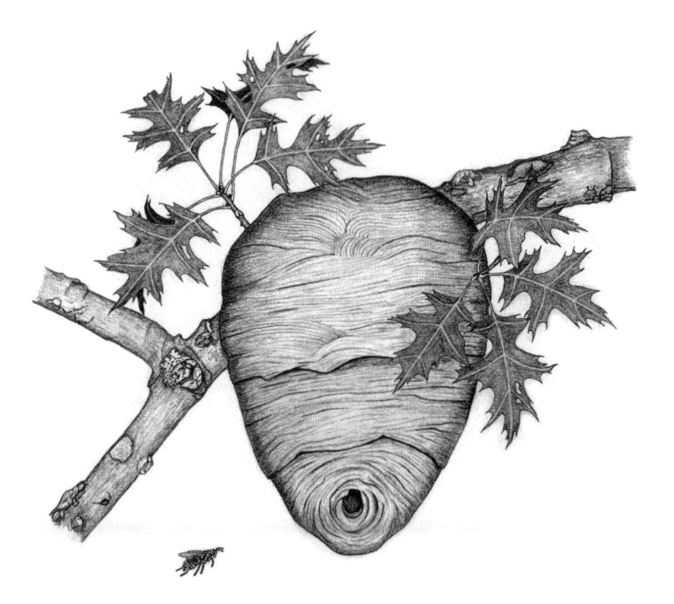

pulp, she "moves back to the original point of application and then works the wet pulp into a flatter, more uniform strip." She repeats this process until she has produced a sufficiently thin strip of paper, which will dry in a minute or two. The paper in a nest is made up of a patchwork of narrow, crescent-shaped strips of different colors—gray if the worker collected fibers from weather-worn wood, various shades of brown or chestnut if she collected fibers of decayed wood, and almost white if her source of fiber was one of certain nonwoody plants.

Paper would be much less useful if there were no ink to write letters and to print books, newspapers, and magazines—even those pesky sales catalogues that clutter our mailboxes every Christmas season. Even money is

Above: In winter, after leaves have fallen, large hornet nests made of paper are easily spotted.

printed on paper with ink. Paper and ink are associated in our minds. If someone were to say *paper* in a word association test, the response would likely be *pen*—and a pen is, of course, an instrument for putting ink on paper. You may be surprised to learn that certain insects have been essential to the production of most kinds of ink since the days of the ancient Greeks in the fifth century B.C.E. The insects in question are tiny wasps that cause the tumorlike growths called galls to develop on plants—particularly on oak trees. An extract of these galls is the most important ingredient of most permanent inks.

"Let there be gall enough in thy ink." These words are spoken in Shakespeare's *Twelfth Night* by Sir Toby, who is advising Sir Andrew to write a letter challenging his competitor for the love of a lady to a duel. Unknown to them, the competitor is actually a woman disguised as a man—making the challenge a futile effort. Nevertheless, Sir Andrew is told to "taunt him with the license of ink" and is counseled with those famous words, quoted above. This familiar quotation has a clever double entendre. *Gall* has two different

Above: A bald-faced hornet adds wood pulp to a sheet of paper on the outside of its nest.

meanings in English. Actually, it is two different words. One is from the Latin *galla,* meaning the plant galls caused by insects, and is a reference to the ink with which Sir Andrew will write his letter. The other, from the Old English *gealla,* means bile or wrath, suggesting the threatening boldness with which Sir Andrew is counseled to frame his challenge.

The anomalous, tumorlike plant growths known as galls may be caused by viruses, bacteria, fungi, certain worms, or mites. But most are caused by insects—perhaps as many as thirteen thousand species of them, according to P. J. Gullan and P. S. Cranston. Gall-making insects, like most plant-feeding insects, tend to be fussy feeders, utilizing only a few closely related plants and usually only a specific part of a plant: leaf, stem, bud, flower, or root. Generally speaking, a given gall maker forms a gall characteristic of its species, and the specific identity of the gall maker can often be determined

---

Above: A tiny wasp that causes the formation of the oak apple, a gall that may be as large as 2 inches in diameter, on the leaves of oak trees.

from just the form of the gall and the plant structure and species of plant on which it is located. Among the insects that cause galls are some species of aphids, thrips, weevils (snout beetles), and moths. But we learn from Arthur Weis and May Berenbaum that about 70 percent of the seventeen hundred North American species of gall-making insects belong to two groups: a family of flies (Cecidomyiidae) and a family of gall wasps (Cynipidae), the latter the insects that form the galls used to make ink.

The insect origin of galls was unknown until the seventeenth century, when it was independently discovered by the English Martin Lister and the Italian Marcello Malpighi. Margaret Fagan comments:

> For centuries before the real origin of insect galls was known, they were noted and given a place, like most other vegetable substances, among remedies for diseases. The ignorance of their origin gave rise to queer superstitions and practices even among scholars, especially in the Middle Ages, when they were gravely recorded as supernatural growths and employed as a means of foretelling the events of the coming year. The gall was supposed to contain a maggot, a fly, or a spider, each of which betokened some misfortune. If the inhabitant were a maggot the coming year would bring famine, if a fly, war, or if a spider, pestilence. This belief was recorded and practiced for several centuries, even after the time of Malpighi, who was the first in the Western World to discover and make known the true origin of insect galls.

The formation of a gall caused by a gall wasp begins after a female has used her sharp, piercing ovipositor (egg-laying organ) to insert a single egg into a specific structure of one of the few plants preferred by her species. The gall wasps are inflexibly host plant–specific. In 1940, Ephraim Felt reported that 750 of the 805 then-known American gall wasps use only oaks. They are equally fussy about choosing the part of the plant into which they will insert the egg. About 32 percent choose a leaf, 22 percent a twig or some other woody part, and the rest lay their eggs on the roots, buds, flowers, or acorns. All of the many species of the genus *Cynips*, a subdivision of the gall wasp family, prefer oaks, according to Alfred Kinsey, but just a few of these trees are used by any one species and not the same ones by all species. Almost all *Cynips* insert their eggs into a leaf.

(Alfred Kinsey merits a parenthetical note. Although he is most famous for his studies of human sexual behavior, he began his career as an entomologist and was the foremost expert on the gall wasp genus *Cynips*. In 1929, he published a five-hundred-page scientific monograph, which is still useful, on the ninety-three species of this genus then known in the United States. In 1942, he became the director of Indiana University's Institute for Sex Research, and ultimately published the famous Kinsey Reports, *Sexual Behavior in the Human Male* [1948] and *Sexual Behavior in the Human Female* [1953].)

The development of a gall and its specific characteristics entails an interaction between the insect, which secretes the gall-inducing stimulus, and the plant, which responds by altering its usual growth pattern. Galls vary in size, shape, and other characteristics, but a gall wasp always stimulates the growth of a gall recognizably typical of its species, and in many cases the species of the gall maker can be determined by the characteristics of its gall. For example, *Cynips* galls on leaves have, varying with the species, many different shapes. Among them are the familiar "oak apple," a smooth-walled sphere that may be as big as a Ping-Pong ball; a smaller sphere covered with short spines like a hedgehog; and a long, thin, hornlike excrescence.

"After many exciting events which occur within this growth," writes Brian Hocking of the gall wasp, "it will eventually, unless it is first seized upon by some avaricious ink-maker, yield another [gall wasp] who will leave a small round hole in its surface as witness to her departure." It isn't always—perhaps not even usually—that simple. Most galls that I have kept in glass jars in my laboratory yielded wasps of several different species—often five or six and sometimes a dozen or more. One of them may have been the gall maker, but some of the others were probably freeloaders that were feeding on the tissues in somebody else's gall, and yet others may have been parasites of the gall maker or of the freeloaders, or perhaps even parasites of the parasites.

Galls of different species—usually made up of concentric layers of several different tissues—are likely to be structurally different internally as well as externally. Kinsey described in detail an especially complex gall that he believed to consist of five layers, although other entomologists recognize only four layers. Surrounding the hollow cell in which the larva lives is the nutritive layer, rich in proteins, sugars, and fats, on which it feeds. Surrounding the nutritive layer is a hard protective layer that is, in turn, surrounded by a layer of spongy tissue, which Kinsey considered to be two separate layers. Finally, there is the outer wall of the gall, which may be smooth or bear outgrowths such as hairs or spines.

Ink was being used to write on parchment and papyrus at least two hundred years before paper was invented by the Chinese in the third century B.C.E. As early as the fifth century B.C.E., Hocking tells us, the Greeks "knew well the properties of gall-nuts which, when extracted with boiling water, yield a solution which turns an inky black on mixture with iron dissolved in acid. This product... has been the principal writing ink of commerce for over two thousand years." Knowledge of gallnut ink spread widely; Fagan notes that this ink was well known in medieval Europe, where monks of the ninth and tenth centuries used it in copying their manuscripts.

Cowan explains that "the galls of commerce, commonly called *Nut-galls,* are found on the *Quercus infectoria,* a species of oak growing in the Levant [the Middle East], and are produced by the *Cynips Gallae-tinctorium* [*sic*].... They are of great importance in the arts, being very extensively used in dyeing and in the manufacture of ink and leather." This gall, commonly known as the Aleppo gall, after the city in Syria, is to this day collected commercially in the Middle East, although at a greatly reduced level. Like cochineal, it has been largely replaced by synthetic products.

Boiling the Aleppo gall—or any oak gall—in water extracts tannin, the concentration of which is unusually high in this gall: 65 percent, according to Felt. Dissolving iron in acid produces salts of iron, such as the iron sulfate that is commonly mixed with a tannin solution to produce ink. When applied to paper, the bluish black ink is at first only faintly visible, but darkens in time and also becomes insoluble in water, making it permanent. Dyes are added to the ink to make it darker and to make writing more immediately visible. To this day, tannins are the basis of our modern blue-black inks, but synthetic dyes are the only coloring matter in modern washable and colored inks. Strong light makes the synthetics fade, however.

Gallnut ink became the sine qua non for record keeping. Fagan notes that

> from the ninth century down to the present day [1918], gall-nuts have been included in practically every good ink recipe for black writing and record inks. The Aleppo gall is considered as the best for ink-making, but other important ones are the Morea gall, the Smyrna gall, Marmora gall and Istrian gall, and other good quality galls from France, Hungary, Italy, Senegal and Barbary....
>
> The Massachusetts Record Commission in 1891 made a Report on Record Inks and Paper in which the superiority of gall-nut ink was attested. The ink made from gall-nuts was said to be permanent, if properly made, and to have the advantage that if the writing should fade it could be repeatedly restored by a solution of nut-gall or tannin. Any other coloring matter

substituted in whole or in part for gall-nut and iron solution impairs the quality of the ink.

Fagan goes on to say that gallnuts are the essential component of the best black writing and record inks. The Aleppo gall is specified in the recipes for inks used by the U.S. Treasury, the Bank of England, the German Chancellory, and the Danish government.

The printing process reproduces not only the written word but also pictures—and, as we have all heard, a picture is worth a thousand words. One of the best ways of reproducing pictures is the printing process known as lithography, and the wax secreted by honey bees has an important function in this process. With a lithographic crayon, originally composed of beeswax, an image is drawn on a smooth surface, ideally the polished surface of a slab of lithographic limestone, which is quarried in Bavaria. (It is in these quarries that fossils of *Archaeopteryx*, a "missing link" between reptiles and birds, are found.) The stone is then sponged with water, which wets the stone but is repelled by the greasy waxen image. When a roller wet with oily ink is passed over the stone, the oily ink adheres to the waxen image, but because of the antipathy of grease and water it does not adhere to the wet, bare surface of the stone. A print is made by pressing a sheet of paper against the stone.

In the next chapter we become more intimately acquainted with certain insects—insects that people eat. Like the quarter of the world's population who are Westerners, you probably have never eaten an insect knowingly. People of most other cultures, however, eat insects—usually not because they are starving and desperate for food, but because they like insects and look upon them as a gastronomic treat.

VII Butterflies in Your Tummy

When I arrived at a party given by the entomologists of the Illinois Natural History Survey, I was greeted at the door by one of my hosts carrying a bowl of French-fried caterpillars. They were the big, fat kind commonly known as corn earworms, which you sometimes find under the husks of an ear of sweet corn, munching on the kernels at its tip. Like all of the guests, I was urged to try one. Even though they looked tempting, as crisp and brown as potato chips, I really didn't want to eat one. Like almost all of us in Western culture, I had never intentionally eaten an insect and had no intention of eating one then. But with some urging, I finally took one and with considerable trepidation popped it into my mouth. It was crispy and delicious! Like many of the other guests, I came back for more. French-fried caterpillars can be at least as addictive as popcorn.

Both the ancient Greeks and Romans regularly ate insects. According to Vincent Holt, the Greeks were particularly fond of the delicate flavor of cicadas, especially females "heavy with their burden of eggs." The Roman epicures "were in the habit of fattening for the table the larvae of [a large

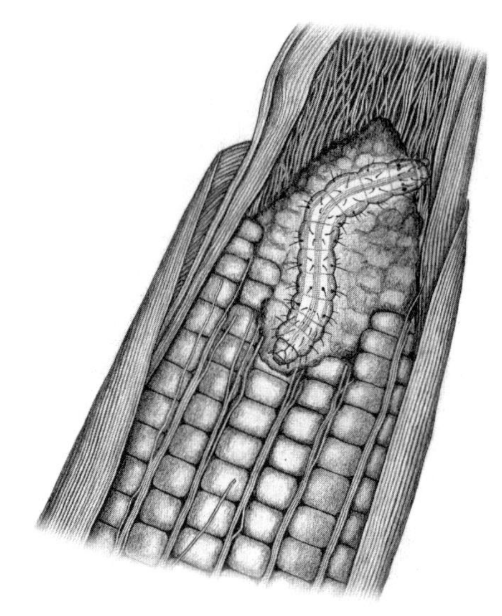

beetle] with flour and wine." The Bible advises the Israelites that "these may ye eat of all winged creeping things that go upon all fours, which have legs above their feet, wherewith to leap upon the earth; even these of them ye may eat: the locust after its kind, and the bald locust after its kind, and the cricket after its kind, and the grasshopper after its kind" (Leviticus 11:21–22). This is a pragmatic exception to the biblical prohibition of the Old Testament against eating all other "winged creeping things"—pragmatic because in the Middle East recurring plagues of locusts, eating almost every green thing, destroy crops. Why not, in a time of famine, eat the locusts that destroyed the crops? Locusts in plagues are so astronomically abundant that large quantities are easily gathered, they

Above: A corn earworm, the caterpillar stage of a moth, munches on the kernels at the tip of an ear of sweet corn.

can be dried and stored, and they are nutritious and delicious if properly cooked.

Today, however, the people of Western culture have a baseless and inexplicable prejudice, just as I had, against the eating of insects, considering them unclean, disgusting, and abhorrent as food. The condescending and offensive words of Herbert Noyes, writing in 1937, are but one of the many expressions of this prejudice: "Before man arrived at his present stage of evolution and was able to realize and appreciate the paramount importance of his status in the Cosmos, he ate termites. His black, less cultured... relatives are doing the same today." We cannot help but wonder how this prejudice arose. After all, our culture, tempered by the words of the Bible, arose from the ancient Greek and Roman civilizations, whose members did eat and relish insects. And we do eat and enjoy lobsters, crayfish, crabs, and shrimp—joint-legged arthropod relatives of the insects that can be thought of as seagoing bugs. Furthermore, the Chinese, the Japanese, and people of many cultures besides our own relish insects as delicious and nutritious food. Richard Vane-Wright, an English entomologist, reports that in Africa his three-year-old daughter found fried mopani worms, large caterpillars, to be irresistible. He does note, though, that her food preferences had yet to be circumscribed by Western prejudices.

In 1885, Holt told a revealing story that illustrates the intensity and pervasiveness of our prejudice against the eating of insects. The book of Mark (3:1, 4) tells us that the food of John the Baptist was locusts and honey. Some biblical scholars, in keeping with their prejudice, went to great lengths to try to prove that the man who baptized Jesus could not have done the unthinkable by eating what was, in their view, such an abhorrent creature as a locust. Despite the well-known fact that the peoples of the Middle East to this day relish locusts as a delicious food, these scholars made long, convoluted, and specious arguments that the word that had been translated as "locust" ought to have been translated as "the edible seed pod of the carob tree." Years later, J. Bequaert was informed by a Greek Orthodox priest that the word *locust* had never been taken by his church as referring to anything other than a grasshopper, and the priest even laughed at the idea of anyone taking it to mean a plant.

The unreasonableness of the Western prejudice against eating insects becomes all too apparent if we contrast the responses of Middle Eastern and American farmers to the famine that results from an invasion of migratory locusts. (In the nineteenth century, a migratory locust—now extinct—often devastated the crops of midwestern farmers.) Charles Valentine Riley, one of the great early American entomologists, reported that after a devastating locust plague in 1874, many people in Kansas and Nebraska were literally "brought to the brink of the grave by sheer lack of food, while the St. Louis papers reported cases of actual death from starvation in some sections of Missouri." Even in the face of starvation, the American farmers—ignoring the words of their Bibles—did not consider eating locusts. Riley did argue in favor of eating locusts, although he well knew that he would be greeted with ridicule, mirth, and even disgust by the very people who were threatened by starvation.

But are insects really a nutritious food for people? The fact that some mammals and birds thrive on a diet of nothing but insects suggests that they are. Keep in mind that the nutritional requirements of all animals, including humans, are basically the same, with variations in the proportions of protein, carbohydrates, and fats and with some minor variations in their requirements for vitamins and minerals. Take, for example, the chimney swifts that flit and soar over our cities. During the daylight hours they are

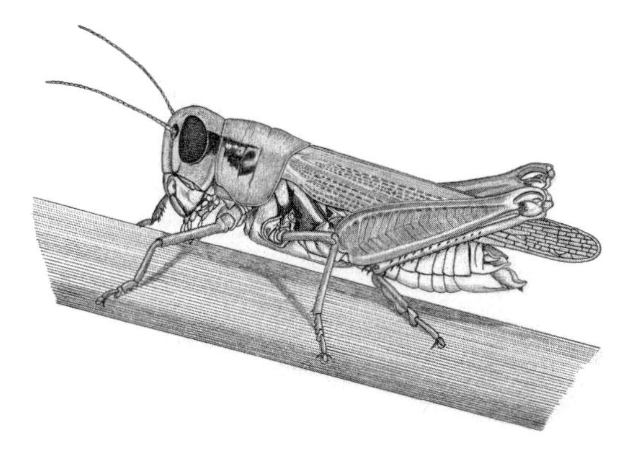

almost constantly on the wing; the large amount of energy they expend is supplied by a diet of nothing but the insects they snap up from the air. The aardvark of Africa grows to a weight of 130 pounds on a diet that includes virtually nothing other than ants and termites. Most seed-eating birds, such as finches, feed their rapidly growing nestlings only insects, although the parents stay on their own vegetarian diet even during the breeding season. (Josselyn van Tyne, an ornithologist, saw a cardinal with its beak full of caterpillars stop at a bird feeder, lay down the caterpillars, and eat some sunflower seeds. Then it retrieved the caterpillars and flew to its nest to feed the caterpillars to its young.)

Generally speaking, insects are a good source of vitamins and minerals. They usually contain sufficient fats and carbohydrates to supply the caloric needs of most animals, and they are also rich in protein, the nutrient most likely to be in short supply in a diet. According to Ronald Taylor, the protein content of raw beef, chicken, and halibut is about 18, 22, and 21 percent,

---

Above: A red-legged grasshopper, a close relative of the now-extinct migratory locust of North America, perches on a stem of big bluestem, a native grass of the American prairies.

respectively, while that of three of the most commonly eaten insects is somewhat greater: raw termites, locusts, and silkworm pupae contain about 23, 31, and 23 percent, respectively.

Although a few insects are poisonous or otherwise unsuitable as food, keep in mind what Gene DeFoliart wrote in 1992: "The long history of human use suggests, however, with little evidence to the contrary, that the insects intentionally harvested for human consumption do not pose any significant health problem." Also keep in mind that we are not dissuaded from eating fruits and vegetables by our knowledge that some plants are poisonous.

In any case, we all eat insects without knowing it. It can't be avoided. Almost all foods contain a few insects or insect fragments, because there is no practical way to exclude all insects while a crop is grown, harvested, shipped, stored, and processed. It might be possible to produce a bottle of ketchup, for example, that contains not so much as one insect fragment, but that would require an all but impossible effort that would increase the price of ketchup astronomically—possibly to hundreds of dollars per bottle. Well aware of this, the U.S. Food and Drug Administration (FDA) does not make the unrealistic demand that foods be completely free of insect "contamination." The FDA has, instead, set a legal limit on how many insects or insect fragments a food may legally contain. For example, 100 grams (3.5 ounces) of frozen broccoli may contain up to sixty aphids, and peanut butter may contain up to thirty insect fragments per 100 grams. These limits, or tolerance levels, are regularly published in *Food Defect Action Levels* by the Department of Health and Human Services.

Among Westerners, there are just a few exceptions to the prejudice against eating insects. In an extensive review article published in 1999, DeFoliart observes that "even Westerners, when exposed to some of the favorite traditional foods of indigenous populations, often become enthusiasts." He presents several examples. In recent years in Australia, he observes, there has been an explosion of interest in "bush tucker," the food of the indigenous Aborigines, which includes many insects. "Bush foods are increasingly appealing to hotel and restaurants frequented by tourists," and are on the menus of posh restaurants in Sydney. Among the favorite insect foods is the witchety "grub," which, according to Ron Cherry, is actually a very large wood-boring caterpillar (genus *Xylentes*) of the carpenter moth family. According to Norman Tindale, "When it is lightly cooked in hot ashes its flavour would delight a gourmet."

Turning to the Western Hemisphere, DeFoliart tells us that "the leaf-cutter ants . . . , known as *hormigas culonas* or big-bottomed ants, are a national delicacy [in Colombia], equivalent in price and gastronomic value with Russian caviar or French truffles." Many believe that these ants, when toasted, are the "highest attainment of Colombian cookery." As long ago as the sixteenth century, the Spanish conquistadores, after overcoming their initial revulsion, became very fond of these toasted ants.

The indigenous people of Mexico ate many different kinds of insects before the Spanish conquest, and they still do. Mexicans of European extraction have developed a taste for some of these insects. "Edible insects," notes DeFoliart, "are not only prominent in the rural markets, but some species command high prices in Mexico City and other urban areas, where they are purchased by people of various economic levels and are sold as delicacies in the restaurants." Among the more popular insect foods are the immature stages, mainly pupae, of the ants known as *escamoles.* Served fried with onions and garlic, they are said to be indescribably delicious. "They are eaten by people of all social classes in Mexico and are considered such a special treat that they are the subjects of songs, dances, and festivities,"

DeFoliart reports. Restaurants in Mexico City charge as much as $25 per plate for *escamoles.* These ants are exported to the United States, Japan, and elsewhere. In Canada, a can containing slightly more than an ounce sold for Canadian $50 (more than U.S. $30) in 1988.

According to an Associated Press feature that appeared in the *Champaign-Urbana News Gazette* of June 23, 2005, in upscale restaurants in Mexico City, deep-fried maguey worms served with a dollop of guacamole sold for as much as $40 a dozen. This "worm" is actually the caterpillar stage of a skipper butterfly that tunnels in the long, swordlike leaves of the maguey plant, also known as the agave or century plant. The sap of the maguey, fermented and distilled, becomes tequila, the main ingredient of a margarita. Traditionally, one of these caterpillars is placed in each bottle of tequila to "prove" that it's the real thing. A helpful clerk in a local liquor store confirmed that some bottles of tequila still contain a caterpillar. In fact, one brand of tequila, he pointed out, has two caterpillars per bottle. Its brand name is Dos Gusanos (Two Worms). Sometimes distillers cheat, and the worm in the bottle is not a maguey caterpillar—sometimes it is not a caterpillar at all.

In both ancient and modern Mexico, the eggs of water boatmen, aquatic insects, were and are still regularly sold in the markets of Mexico City. In the lakes around the city, notes W. E. China, some water boatmen are so astronomically abundant that they and their eggs are a common and plentiful food for humans. As Friedrich Bodenheimer reports, when bundles of rushes are placed in shallow water, these insects immediately begin laying eggs on them. About a month later, the bundles—each encrusted with thousands of eggs—are taken out of the water, dried, and then beaten on a cloth to knock off the dried eggs. China writes that they "are either cooked alone . . . or mixed with meal and made into cakes which are eaten with green chiles."

The people of modern Asian countries, including the Japanese and Chinese, have no prejudice against the eating of insects. Many different kinds of insects are eaten throughout eastern Asia by people of all classes, usually as an epicurean treat rather than as a staple eaten out of necessity. These people eat insects because they like them.

Take, for example, the giant water bug, which may be as much as 3 inches long, and which itself eats aquatic insects and even small fish. Giant water bugs are regularly eaten by the people of Myanmar (Burma), China, India, Indonesia, Laos, Thailand, and Vietnam. In 1969, Robert Pemberton saw large quantities of these bugs being gathered during their dispersal flights in a rice-growing area in Thailand. According to W.S. Bristowe, this bug, known as *mangda* in Thai, is a great delicacy that "reaches the tables of princes in Bangkok." The *mangda* may be steamed, soaked in shrimp sauce, and then picked apart and eaten much as we eat a crab. It is said to taste like gorgonzola cheese. Pemberton, who found *mangda* on sale for $1.50 each in a Thai market in Berkeley, California, says that Thais make a condiment, *nam prik mangda,* by "combining and mashing a whole bug with salt, sugar, garlic, shallots, fish sauce, lime juice, and hot Thai capsicum

Above: A bottle of Mexican mescal containing a maguey worm, which was found feeding on a maguey, or agave, plant.

peppers in a mortar and pestle." This paste is commonly used as a vegetable dip and as a topping for cooked rice.

The Japanese, ultramodern and consummately civilized, eat insects as a delicacy, a special treat. DeFoliart, writing in 1999, reported: "In both historical and modern Japan, the most popular and widely eaten insects have been the rice-field grasshoppers . . . which, fried and slightly seasoned with soy sauce, are known as *inago.*" When I was with the army of occupation in Tokyo in 1946 and 1947, street vendors of produce displayed large baskets of dried grasshoppers. This was before DDT and the other "miracle insecticides" were widely used. Later, their use made these grasshoppers rare. But with the decreasing use of pesticides in recent years, the grasshoppers' population is on the increase, and "inago is reappearing on dinner tables and in supermarkets and restaurants, although it is still sold as a luxury item."

Bee or wasp larvae, *hachinoko,* are a close second to *inago* as a luxury food in modern Japan. A Japanese professor of zoology described to Charles Remington one of the ways in which wasp larvae and pupae are collected. A small charge of gunpowder is pushed into the underground nest with a long stick. After the fuse is lit and the gunpowder explodes, the wasps are stunned and do not sting. Only then are the larvae and pupae collected. They may be eaten raw or cooked in soy sauce and served on rice. A Japanese author quoted by DeFoliart reported that in 1987 the terminally ill Emperor Hirohito finished a dish of wasp larvae and rice even when he refused most of the other dishes he was offered. According to Pemberton and Yamasaki, in 1990 a can of wasp larvae, "child hornets," weighing about 3.5 ounces sold for $20 in the prestigious Mitsukoshi department store in Tokyo. They comment that "these insects and other old foods keep an earlier Japan alive and available, even in Tokyo amongst the glass and steel towers and the fast food restaurants."

In much of Asia, probably almost everywhere that silk is produced, the pupae that remain after the silk has been unwound from the cocoon are not wasted. They are eaten. Ronald Taylor noticed that a pleasant odor of food being cooked permeated a factory where cocoons were being unwound. The odor was present because, as you know, the silk cannot be reeled from the cocoons unless they are first dropped into very hot water, and that is enough to cook the pupae within them. "Thus the girls who unreel the silk," Taylor relates, "have a plentiful supply of freshly cooked food before them, which they eat intermittently during the long hours of their working day."

The many pupae that don't become snacks for the girls are marketed as fresh food or are preserved, usually by drying, for future consumption. In either case, they are looked on as a special treat. Fresh pupae, Taylor observes, are prepared in various ways. They may be fried in fat and seasoned with "lemon" leaves or salt. A reportedly tasty soup is made by boiling them in water with cabbage. Dried pupae, Bodenheimer tells us, are first softened in water and may then be prepared in an omelet with chicken eggs or simply fried with onions and sauce.

Silkworm pupae are not a trivial resource. Every year in India, dried defatted silkworm pupae are ground to produce more than 22,000 tons of meal, which is eaten by people or fed to poultry. As DeFoliart reports, the pupae are rich in protein: 63 percent in dried pupae and about 75 percent in the meal made from defatted pupae.

The Western prejudice against eating insects has two unfortunate consequences. The first and less important is that it deprives Westerners of the opportunity to partake of some truly delicious and nutritious foods. The second, but by far the more serious consequence, is that poorly fed people of third world countries are reluctant, if not altogether unwilling, to continue the tradition of eating insects, because they are influenced by *our* prejudice, communicated to them by Westerners such as missionaries and administrative officers. In Africa, according to DeFoliart, the more educated natives are reluctant to admit that the eating of insects and other traditional customs still exist among the indigenous people. Similarly, in Papua New Guinea the people "are coming to believe that eating insects is 'bush behavior' to be discarded in their progress toward development," DeFoliart writes. My physician, a native of Nigeria, told me that his grandmother fed him termites, but he has not eaten them since. In Zimbabwe, a few people are refusing to eat caterpillars, a traditional food, because they have been told that caterpillars are food for "primitives."

The eating of insects is a long-standing tradition among many of the so-called primitive people of the world. Insects are an important part of their diet even if they are eaten in relatively small quantities. Rich in nutrients, even a small serving of caterpillars or some other insect may supply a significant percentage of the protein required by people to whom meat and fish are seldom or almost never available. In the Democratic Republic of the Congo as a whole, 20 percent of the available animal protein in the human diet is supplied by insects, and in some areas of the country as much as 64 percent. In Zambia, caterpillars constitute as much as 40 percent of the available animal protein during the "hungry months," November to February. In Papua New Guinea, insects supply as much as 30 percent of the people's requirement for protein.

Insects probably have been an important part of the diet of most, if not virtually all, of the so-called primitive peoples of the world, including Native Americans. According to the little information available, worldwide at least seven hundred different kinds of insects are eaten by people. But the actual number is without doubt far greater. After all, tens of thousands of the nine hundred thousand species of insects currently known to science are probably both edible and palatable.

Native Americans must have eaten many kinds of insects before they were conquered and acculturated by Europeans. Some still do. In historical times, the Indians of Utah gathered hundreds of bushels of the many billions of edible aquatic brine fly pupae that washed up on the beaches of the Great Salt Lake. The Modoc Indians of California, according to Bodenheimer, shook snipe flies that gathered in large masses on overhanging foliage into the Pitt River, trapping the floating flies and masses of their eggs downstream against a barrier of floating logs. As many as one hundred bushels could be harvested in a single day.

"There are modern Indian people in the United States, living within walking distance of major grocery and fast food chains," report Elizabeth Blake and Michael Wagner, "who choose to collect and eat larvae of the Pandora moth.... These large, heavy-bodied caterpillars, that can be more than 2 inches long, are known as *piuga* to the Paiute Indians of California and are one of their traditional foods." These caterpillars, which feed on the needles of several western pines, are available only every second year because of their biennial life cycle. With the onset of cold weather in their first year, the partly grown caterpillars stop feeding and aggregate in clusters on the branches of their tree. The following spring, they resume feeding, and, in the second or third week of July, when full-grown, they crawl down the trunk of the tree to molt to the pupal stage in a shallow burrow in the soil. The Paiutes trap the descending larvae in shallow trenches that encircle the tree. Every few hours the caterpillars are gathered and baked for about an hour in a pile of sand that has been heated by heaping it with burning wood. Then they are sifted from the sand and laid out on a tarpaulin to dry for up to two weeks. In the old days, the dried *piuga* were stored in small lean-to shelters in a cool, dry place for from one to two years. Today they are stored in a freezer. The dry, roasted larvae are boiled in plain or salted water for about an hour to soften them and are then eaten as finger food. The harvest can be plentiful. In 1920, according to J. M. Aldrich, a group of Paiutes collected and processed 1.5 tons of *piuga.*

The Australian Aborigines relied heavily, and to a lesser extent still do, on insects as food, possibly more so than any other group of hunter-gatherers. "Every Aboriginal," Tindale writes, "is constantly on the watch for insect food. I have seen a man, who supposedly was engrossed in the stalking of a kangaroo, glance aside at a likely gum tree and turn away from the hunt to test a hole with his spear-point. This led him to make a hooked stick with which he pulled out a grub. . . . He ate it and only then did his attention return to the more serious business of the hunt." The Aborigines ate a wide variety of insects and sometimes still eat some of them: the larvae of wood-boring beetles, and the adults and caterpillars of several species of moths, ants, and locusts. The Aborigines also exploit some insect products: the honey of the stingless bees and the honeypot ants and the honeydew produced by the jumping plant lice (family Psyllidae), all of which you will meet in chapter 8.

Among the many caterpillars consumed by the Aborigines, the most widely known are the huge wood-boring caterpillars known as witchety "grubs." The females of several species of this genus, Tindale notes, share the record of being the heaviest insect in the world. The adult females have an impressive wingspan of 9 inches. The full-grown caterpillars are hefty and as long as a man's hand. The keen-eyed Aborigines, according to Bodenheimer, spot the holes made by the caterpillars in the trunk of eucalyptus trees and extract them with a hooked stick about 6 inches long made from a forked twig, "one arm of which is left the required length, and the other cut short and sharpened to form the hook." Because the hole's entrance may not be wide enough for the caterpillar to pass through, "the bark is first cut away to a small depth with a tomahawk." The plump caterpillars, said to have the flavor of "scrambled eggs, slightly sweetened," are cooked by roasting them on hot ashes.

The ghost moths (family Hepialidae), rather large and narrow-winged, resemble our common night-flying sphinx moths. In the caterpillar stage, some species live underground chewing on the roots of eucalyptus or acacia trees. Tindale explains how Aborigines collect the caterpillars: "[They] have learned to detect trees which have been debilitated by the attacks of hepialid larvae, and scrape off the surface soil, exposing the tunnels. They test the holes by smell; the humid ones are those containing living larvae and pupae. A long supple stick with a hook at its lower end is worked carefully down the holes, sometimes to the astonishing depth of 6 feet. The creature is hooked and pulled up." Tindale comments that this is "a slow and tedious business," and that "a better way to enjoy a feast of Ghost Moths is to wait until the season of emergence of the adults." In the deserts of Australia, the moths emerge from the ground en masse an hour before dusk on the day of the first big rain of summer. They begin to fly, mate, and lay eggs when it gets dark. By morning, the moths—dead or exhausted—lie on the ground. "On the eve of a flight birds seem to be aware of an unusual event. Magpies and crows are active, and owls and mopokes leave their shelters earlier than usual to feed on the moths. At first the moths hang limp and helpless, drying their wings in the twilight. Aborigines are never far behind. Hundreds of the moths are gathered into dillybags and, as soon as it is dark, large fires are lit into which the moths crash in great numbers, to be raked out and eaten by the eager diners."

As already noted, the people of northern Africa relish locusts. They also eat certain beetles. For example, Bristowe notes that the Bedouins of Egypt eat scarab beetles roasted in salt and that these beetles play a part in their coming-of-age ceremony:

> When a boy reaches the age of 11 or 12 a ceremony initiating him to manhood takes place which has been described to me by Miss F. Finch from personal observation, as follows: A circle of men squatting on the ground surrounds the boy and a Sheikh. The men are shoulder to shoulder each touching his neighbour on either side of him. They chant in rhythm the 99 names of Allah, swaying from side to side and working themselves up to a pitch of great excitement. In less than half an hour, the men composing the circle and the boy seated in the centre are in a kind of trance. The Sheikh who has remained relatively calm and unaffected then reads extracts from the Koran relating to eternal life and commands the boy to eat from a bowl which contains scarabs, and the boy is then recognized as a man of the tribe or village.

But south of the Sahara Desert, insects of many more species have been widely used as food, among them locusts, other grasshoppers, beetle larvae (grubs), termites, ants, caterpillars, dragonfly nymphs, bee and wasp larvae and pupae, and the adult form of the tiny flies known as midges.

In 1921, Bequaert noted that the "Hottentots" (that is, the Khoikhoi) of the Kalahari Desert in southern Africa rejoice when a swarm of migratory locusts appears. They ascribe the arrival of this welcome food to the goodwill of a spirit who lives far to the north and removes a rock to release the locusts from a deep pit. The grateful people gorge on them and after "a few days they grow visibly fatter and appear in a much better state of health." During the dry season, swarms of tiny midges so dense that they look like clouds of smoke emerge from central African lakes. When they are driven landward by the wind, huge quantities of them are swept off bushes and rocks by the people and compressed into oily cakes, roasted, and eaten.

In much of Africa, termites are considered to be one of the most—if not *the* most—delicious of foods. The sub-Saharan Africans' fondness for termites is picturesquely conveyed by Herbert Noyes: "As a Bayere chief, who, calling on Dr. Livingstone, was offered apricot jam, remarked: 'Ah, you should try toasted termites.' So, in Central Africa, natives welcome the rainy season [when termites swarm] in very much the same way as obese British gourmands hail the advent of the oyster season and journey from afar to gorge themselves at Colchester on living food."

The termites that are most often eaten are of species that build mounds, which may be several feet tall. At the beginning of the rainy season, a colony releases thousands—more likely tens of thousands or more—of the winged members of the reproductive caste to found new colonies. Both Bequaert and Bodenheimer describe an ingenious trap for collecting large numbers of these winged reproductives as they leave the mound. According to Bodenheimer: "They [the trappers] tightly enfold the termite mound in several . . . broad leaves . . . the interstices soon being closed by the termites, which usually join the inner leaves to the nest. A projecting pocket, built on one side of the leaf cover, serves as a trap; for when the winged termites begin to swarm, they find no egress and finally drop in masses into the pocket from which they are scooped out." The termites are eaten raw, boiled, broiled, or roasted in an iron pot. In Zimbabwe, DeFoliart tells us, many people of European origin eat termites—but not as much as the natives do.

Native children catch termites by poking a palm leaf into a hole in a mound that has been broken open. They withdraw it to eat the termites that cling to it. This is much like Jane Goodall's account of the way chimpanzees catch termites. She notes that while the winged reproductives await suitable flying conditions, the termites excavate passages through the walls of the mound and lightly seal the openings. When a chimpanzee sees one of these sealed holes, it uses its index finger to scratch away the seal. Then it literally makes a tool by, for example, picking a thin twig, stripping it of leaves, and breaking it to a convenient length of about 9 inches. The tool is poked into the hole and withdrawn. The termites clinging to it with their mandibles are removed by drawing the twig, stem of grass, or other material used to make the tool "sideways through the mouth."

People of all cultures have a sweet tooth, and often satisfy that craving by eating honey, which is made not only by bees but also by ants and wasps. As you will see next, the cooperative collecting of nectar by honey bees is feasible because they communicate with one another by means of an authentic language, and the conversion of nectar into honey is accomplished by a rather complex process that, over the millennia, has been honed to perfection by natural selection, the driving force of evolution.

VIII Satisfying the Sweet Tooth

Honey was virtually the only sweet available to the people of Europe and North Africa for thousands of years until sugar cane was brought to the Mediterranean area from China. We learn from Eva Crane that nine thousand years ago, during the middle Stone Age, a primitive artist drew a picture in a rock shelter in Spain of a person robbing honey from a nest of wild bees. In ancient Egypt, according to Percy Newberry, honey was so highly prized that

> two important officials of the oldest period ... were closely concerned with the use of the seal, and their titles were derived from its name. One of these was the "Sealer of the Honey [jars]"; the other was the "Divine Sealer," "Sealer of the God." The first title ... "the Sealer of the Honey [jars]," was, perhaps, the oldest of the many hundreds of titles that we find at all periods of Egyptian history, and from the Third Dynasty onwards there was probably not a man of less than royal rank who would not have been proud to bear it. It originally meant, as we have said, "the Sealer of the Honey [jars]," honey being the greatest of all primitive luxuries, and its use reserved for the king's table. This title must therefore be regarded as a relic of the most extreme

> antiquity, and it certainly goes back to the time before the use of wine in the Nile Valley.

The Third Dynasty began about five thousand years ago, and the use of honey probably predates that by many centuries, going back to the most extreme antiquity.

Honey, notes Holley Bishop, is frequently mentioned in the Rig-Veda, the sacred Hindu scriptures, which dates from roughly 1500 B.C.E. Homer's *Odyssey* and *Iliad,* dating back almost three thousand years, are, as Bishop so nicely puts it, "liberally sweetened with references to sacred bees and their blessed [honey]." In Book XIV of the *Odyssey,* Homer speaks of "wine yet new,/And luscious as the bees' nectarous dew." Honey is also referred to in the Bible. In the Old Testament, Jehovah repeatedly promises Moses—who lived about 1400 B.C.E.—that the Israelites wandering in the desert would come to a land of milk and honey. King Solomon rhapsodized about the beauty of his beloved Shulamite: "Thy lips, O my bride, drop as the honeycomb: honey and milk are under thy tongue."

In the book of Judges, we are told a strange tale that reveals how little people actually knew about honey bees and other insects in biblical times. Samson, on his way to claim his intended bride, "turned aside to see the carcass of the lion: and, behold, there was a swarm of bees in the body of the lion, and honey. And he took it into his hands, and went on, eating as he went; and he came to his father and mother, and gave unto them, and they did eat." Honey bees definitely do not nest in the rotting bodies of dead animals. What the ancients actually saw were probably drone flies (*Eristalis tenax*) that bear an uncanny resemblance to a honey bee. By mimicking the appearance of the venomous, stinging, and warningly colored honey bee, these harmless flies trick birds and other insect eaters into passing them up as a meal. The flies, which definitely do not make honey, do, however, "swarm" about the decaying bodies of dead animals—even lions. It is there that they lay their eggs, and the maggots that hatch from them are scavengers that feed on the decaying carcass.

Honey bees make honey—I will soon tell you how—from sweet nectar that they collect from flowers. Bees of all kinds, not only honey bees, play an essential role in the reproduction of the flowers they visit to collect pollen and nectar, their only food. Pollen adheres to a nectar-collecting bee's hairy body when it brushes against the male parts of the flower, and when it visits another flower—almost always, at least in the case of the honey bee, one of the same species as the first flower—some of the pollen rubs off on that second flower's female structures. In this way the bee initiates the process of fertilization and the consequent production of seeds, the plant's offspring. Metabolizing the sugar in the nectar, which contains few other nutrients, releases the energy that fuels the bees' long pollen- and nectar-collecting flights. "Nurse bees" eat a rich diet of pollen and honey to produce bee's milk, secreted from special glands on the head. Bee's milk is a very nutritious food, which they feed to the developing larvae. "A worker larva," reports Ray Snodgrass, "within 4½ to 5 days increases its initial weight 1,500 times."

Flowering plants and the insects that pollinate them—using the honey bee as an example—have coevolved; that is, over millions of years they have adapted to each other in various ways. The large, colorful blossoms of flowering plants attract the bees from a distance, and, correspondingly, the bees have discriminating color vision. (They can see even the ultraviolet part of the spectrum, which is reflected by many blossoms but is invisible to us.) The blossoms also give off scents, and the antennae of the bees bear sensitive odor receptors, which perceive these close-range attractants that distinguish a plant's species. The plants reward the bees with pollen and nectar, and honey bees are very well adapted to take advantage of this bounty. On each hind leg they have a "pollen basket" of stiff bristles that can carry a large load of pollen, and their "honey stomachs" can hold large volumes of nectar, which they collect with specially adapted mouthparts modified for both sucking and lapping.

Honey bees are remarkably efficient collectors of pollen and nectar. The workers of a single colony forage over an area of as much as 40 square miles surrounding their manmade hive or, perhaps, their nest in a hollow tree. Clearly, with such a large area to cover, efficient foraging requires that a scouting worker that finds a productive patch of flowers with abundant nectar and/or pollen be able to communicate its location to other workers. She—all workers are sterile females—accomplishes this by performing a "waggle dance" on the vertical surface of a comb hanging in the nest. This dance maps out the most direct flight line to the productive flowers. Anna Dornhaus and Lars Chittka point out that their dance language gives honey bees a competitive advantage over other bees, such as bumblebees, that have no language and can communicate to their nest mates no more information than that flowers are available at some unspecified place. As the honey bee worker dances, other workers crowd in close and follow her movements. They perceive the distinctive scent of the flower, which clings to her body, and occasionally the dancer gives them a tiny sip of the flower's nectar. The honey bee dancer describes a figure eight, waggling her abdomen from side to side and squeaking as she dances along the crossbar of the figure. The speed of the "waggle run," the crossbar, indicates distance: the slower she moves, the more distant the flowers, and the faster, the closer the flowers.

The direction to the flowers is specified by the angle of the waggle run with respect to the vertical axis of the comb. Just as we follow the convention that the top of a map is north, the bees understand that the top of the comb represents the position of the sun. Hence, if the crossbar runs straight up the comb, the flight line from the hive to the flowers is directly toward the sun; if it runs straight down the comb, the flight line is directly away from the sun. A crossbar that runs up the comb at a 60-degree angle to the right of the vertical indicates that the most direct flight line is 60 degrees to the right of a line from the hive to the sun. One that runs up the comb at an angle 45 degrees to the left indicates that the appropriate flight line is 45 degrees to the left of a line from the hive to the sun. As you would expect, the bees have an internal clock that allows them to compensate for the changing position of the sun as the Earth rotates.

When a worker flies to the indicated patch of flowers and returns to the nest, she repeats the waggle dance—enthusiastically if she found the flowers to be productive—thereby recruiting many more workers that will forage from these flowers. But she does not repeat the dance if the flowers were not productive, or, if they were only marginally productive, dances halfheartedly and recruits few workers. Furthermore, Carl Anderson and Francis Ratnieks found that the returning forager does not dance if she has difficulty in finding house bees to take her load of nectar, an indication that no more nectar is required at that time. In this way, the colony regulates foraging and focuses it on the most productive patches of flowers.

If the source of nectar or pollen is relatively close to the hive or nest, within 60 yards or less, the bees do a simple dance that Karl von Frisch calls the round dance. The returning foraging worker announces her find by running in a circle "with swift, tripping steps," suddenly reversing direction, then returning to her original course, and so on. The message is: "Look around close to our nest and you can't miss the flowers."

Von Frisch, the Nobel laureate who discovered and decoded the honey bees' dance language, demonstrated his understanding of the waggle dance by following the directions the bees gave as they danced on a comb in a glass-fronted observation hive. These bees were visiting a sugar water feeder that von Frisch's students had hidden behind a bush far from the observation hive. By following the directions given by the bees, he found his way to within a few yards of the hidden feeder, and with a bit of searching he found it.

Many beekeepers are more than willing to help out their bees in their quest for nectar. They may move their hives from place to place to take advantage of an abundance of nectar-producing flowers—perhaps a field of clover. In areas where there are apple or citrus orchards, the orchardists rent hives from beekeepers to ensure that the blossoms on their trees will be pollinated. Egyptian beekeepers used a very clever way of bringing their hives to where the flowers were. They realized that flowers blossomed much earlier in Upper (southern) Egypt than in Lower (northern) Egypt. At the end of October, as Hilda Ransome tells us, they moved their hives up the Nile to southern Egypt, where flowers blossomed abundantly at that time. The hives were placed on rafts and, as the season progressed, gradually moved down the river to keep in step with the blossoming of the flowers. They were moored close to the shore, and the bees were released to collect nectar. When the blossoming period ended at that site, the rafts were moved a few miles downstream. In this way they passed through all of Egypt, finally arriving at Cairo at the beginning of February.

How do the bees convert nectar to honey? It all begins, explains Norman Gary, when a "field bee," a forager, returns to the hive or other nest site with her honey stomach full of nectar. She may have sipped nectar from more than a thousand small flowers or from far fewer larger flowers to fill up with

as much as 70 milligrams of nectar, a tiny fraction of an ounce but about 85 percent of her body weight (equivalent to a 150-pound person drinking 127 pounds of water). After the forager enters the nest, she regurgitates the nectar to the stay-at-home "house bees," who begin to "ripen" the nectar to convert it to honey.

This conversion requires the removal of a great deal of water from the nectar and the addition of various enzymes to it. (Enzymes are proteins that promote and regulate biochemical reactions.) One of the many enzymes bees add to nectar splits molecules of the complex sucrose molecule, common table sugar and the most abundant sugar in nectar, into its two component parts, fructose and glucose. These two simple sugars constitute about 70 percent of the sugar content of honey. (The other enzymes have different functions.) In addition to these two sugars, honey also contains

Above: Perched on a waxen comb, a honey bee worker is about to regurgitate nectar into one of the hexagonal cells.

smaller amounts of a number of other sugars, proteins, acids, and minerals and even smaller quantities of vitamins and other substances that give honey its pleasing color, flavor, and aroma.

The house bees are responsible for evaporating most of the water from the nectar delivered by foragers. They repeatedly expose droplets of nectar to the air by regurgitating them and holding them in their mouthparts. They do this about every five to ten seconds for a period of about twenty minutes. After this, the nectar, which initially contained about 45 percent sugar, has lost enough water for its concentration of sugar to have increased to about 60 percent. This partially ripened honey is then placed in cells for additional drying. The cells are only about one-quarter filled, however, because the rate of evaporation is faster in partially filled than in completely filled cells. Some of the house bees fan their wings to circulate air in and out of the nest, thereby hastening evaporation. The fully ripened honey, which has a sugar concentration of about 75 to 85 percent, is consolidated to completely fill cells, which are finally capped with wax.

A jar of honey can sit on your pantry shelf for weeks or months without fermenting or otherwise spoiling—although it may granulate—because microorganisms such as yeasts and bacteria cannot survive in honey. Jason DeMera and Esther Angert found that the honey of both the European honey bees and the stingless bees we will meet later contain chemical substances that kill yeasts and bacteria. Microorganisms probably could not survive in honey even if it contained no such substances, however. The water content of the honey, about 20 percent, is so much lower than that of the microorganisms, about 70 percent, that the microorganisms would dry up in the honey. This is because water, like other liquids and gasses, diffuses from a place of high concentration (a microorganism in this case) to one of low concentration (the honey). Thus, the water is sucked out of the microorganisms by osmosis, leaving behind their dead dry husks. Bishop warns, however, that honey may contain the spores (an inactive resting stage) of the bacteria that produce the toxin botulin. The spores are harmless to adults but may be deadly to infants less than a year old.

If enough water is added to honey, the osmotic pressure is decreased enough so that yeasts can survive in the diluted honey. Yeast causes honey to ferment, and fermentation yields alcohol. By the time of ancient Greece and Rome—and surely much earlier—people were making an alcoholic beverage, a honey wine that is known as mead in English. In *Beowulf,* written down in Old English in about 1100 C.E., mead is the drink of kings and thanes (free landholders). In Chaucer's *Canterbury Tales,* written in Middle English more than two hundred years later and translated into modern English by J. U. Nicolson, we read in the tale of Sir Thopas:

> They brought him, first, the sweet, sweet wine,
> And mead within a maselyn,
> And royal spicery
> Of gingerbread that was full fine,
> Cumin and licorice, I opine,
> And sugar so dainty.

Gingerbread contains honey, and a maselyn, according to Nicolson, is a bowl made of maple wood.

In *Making Mead,* Roger Morse quotes a recipe from a book published in 1669, *The Closet of the Eminently Learned Sir Kenelme Digbie Kt. Opened: Whereby Is Discovered Several Ways for Making of Metheglin, Sider, Cherry Wine, etc.* (Metheglin is spiced mead.)

A RECEIPT FOR MEATHE

To seven quarts of water, take two quarts of honey, and mix it well together; then set it on the fire to boil, and take three or four Parsley-roots, and as many Fennel-roots, and shave them clean, and slice them, and put them into the Liquor, and boil altogether, and skim it very well all the while it is a boyling, and when there will no more scum rise, then it is boiled enough; but be careful that none of the scum do boil into it. Then take it off, and let it cool till the next day. Then put it up in a close vessel, and put thereto half a pint of new good barm [yeast], and a very few Cloves pounded and put in a Linnen-cloth, and tie it in a vessel, and stop it up close; and within a fortnight, it will be ready to drink: but if it stay longer, it will be the better.

The Scottish drink Drambuie is one of my favorite after-dinner liqueurs. It seems, according to Eva Crane's *A Book of Honey,* that I am far from the only lover of Drambuie. She also tells us that the word *drambuie* is said to be a contraction of the Gaelic *an dram buideach,* the drink that satisfies. It is made from a secret recipe that incorporates honey and whiskey. Since 1745, when the recipe was brought to Scotland by Bonnie Prince Charlie, it has been a closely guarded secret passed down from generation to generation of the same family.

Many years ago I swapped yarns with Bob Knight of Dublin, New Hampshire, who told me how he hunted for bee trees, wild colonies of honey bees. He trapped a foraging bee at a flower in a small box divided into three compartments. At one end of the box were two compartments, one above the other. The upper was covered by a removable ceiling, or lid, with a glass window, and the lower, separated from the upper by another lid, contained a piece of honeycomb with sugar water. The third compartment, the other end of the box, had a ceiling with another glass window and was separated from the other two compartments by a sliding panel that could be pulled out of the box through a narrow slit.

Bob trapped a bee in the upper compartment; when it calmed down, he let it move into the third compartment by pulling out the sliding panel and then trapped it in there by pushing the panel back in. Next he removed the lid that separated the upper and lower compartments, giving the bee access to the sugar water in the latter compartment. After feeding on the sugar water, the bee was released. It would make a beeline back to its nest. All the inside walls of the box had been coated with oil of anise. When the bee returned to the nest and did the waggle dance, the other bees perceived the odor of the anise clinging to its body. When they left the nest to go to the feeder that was indicated by the dance, they ignored the scents of flowers along the way and stopped only when they smelled anise. (This "flower constancy" makes honey bees efficient pollinators.) When many bees were visiting his now open box, Bob gradually followed them back to their nest by making short hops along the flight line, letting the bees feed at each stop. Sometimes the bees led him to a beekeeper's hive rather than to a wild colony in a hollow tree. In that case he did not harvest the honey.

Much of the world is now in the midst of a very scary crisis involving western honey bees. They are mysteriously disappearing—at last count an average of about 30 percent from twenty-seven U.S. states and several other countries, perhaps including Brazil. As May Berenbaum told me, "The bees are simply disappearing. There are no bodies. It's as if they're not coming home." Hypotheses to explain this catastrophic loss of the pollinators of our crops and of many wild plants abound. Among the more fanciful proposed causes are jet contrails and the wireless Internet, but a more reasonable one may be the artificial feeding—sometimes necessary—

with high-fructose corn syrup, a nutritionally inadequate food for bees. No matter the cause, the economic and ecological losses resulting from colony collapse disorder will be very serious indeed. The scarcity or even the loss of our honey supply would pain many of us, but as Berenbaum points out, that will be trivial compared to the devastation from lack of pollination. Almost all of our fruits and many of our vegetables are honey bee–pollinated. And almonds, a two-billion-dollar-a-year industry in California, are pollinated only by honey bees. A scarcity of pollinators affects even our meat supply; clovers and other leguminous hay and forage crops are honey bee–pollinated.

Tracking down bee trees was just a hobby for Bob Knight, but in India, Southeast Asia, and the East Indies, harvesting honey from colonies of wild bees was and is a serious business that can be dangerous and even deadly. In this region, according to Benjamin Oldroyd and Siriwat Wongsiri, there are eight species of honey bees (*Apis*) other than our western honey bee (*Apis mellifera*), which—except for its African race—is relatively mild-mannered. There are four species that nest in cavities, as does *mellifera.* One of them has been domesticated on a small scale and is kept in wooden hives. There are four others that build uncovered combs that hang from the underside of a branch or the rocky face of a cliff. The workers of two of the latter four species, the giant honey bees, may be only a little less than twice as long as those of our familiar *mellifera.* They yield the most honey and are by far the most dangerous to deal with. One of them lives in the Himalayas and hangs its single comb from a rock face. Colonies of the other of these two species, which is found in Asia south of the Himalayas, builds a single very large comb that hangs from a rock face or, more commonly, from the underside of a branch of a very tall tree. As with the Himalayan species, large aggregations of their colonies are commonly seen; according to Oldroyd and Wongsiri, two hundred or more colonies may be "crammed onto a single water tower, tree, or rock face."

"Hunting giant bee colonies," say Oldroyd and Wongsiri, "is an extraordinarily hazardous occupation, involving climbing to great heights, often in darkness, and then dealing with tens of thousands of ferocious stinging insects." Beyond the hunt itself, there are other dangers in the forest. For example, in Bangladesh, "tigers killed about 10 honey hunters each year, and another 40 are attacked by bandits." That was, of course, before the Asian tiger was on the verge of extinction. But as far as I know, bandits may still be active. The honey hunters try to mitigate the danger by choosing an auspicious day and by preparing themselves "with ritual washing, fasting, chants, and prayers." They may also offer sacrifices, such as betel nut, rice, or a small animal, to the spirit of the forest. When they arrive at the base of the bee tree, they say prayers and perform rituals to placate the spirit of the tree. According to a Malay legend quoted by Oldroyd and Wongsiri, a young prince who used metal in collecting honey from a nest of giant honey bees in a tualang tree was killed and dismembered by the spirit of the tree. His wife, the Princess Fatima, and the tree made a deal. The prince would be restored to life if, in the future, "no knives or iron implements of any sort will be used when climbing a tualang tree." Respecting Fatima's deal with the tree, most honey hunters from Malaysia to southern India use no metal. They cut the combs with a wooden knife.

Many hunters prefer to raid colonies of giant bees on moonless nights, when the fiercely stinging workers, which are then clinging to the comb, cannot mount an aerial attack. Carrying a torch of bundled leaves more than 4 feet long, the hunter climbs up the bare trunk of a tree to a comb-bearing branch that may be 130 feet above the ground. He then crawls out on the branch to the combs, perhaps for 30 feet or more, lights his torch, and uses it to brush bees from the combs. He will also cause sparks to fall from the tree by hitting the branch with his torch. "Disoriented bees follow the sparks, and the hunter will often chant that the bees 'should follow' the stars."

After clearing the nest of most of its bees, the hunter suspends a basket beneath the comb and reaches down to cut off pieces of honey comb that will be lowered in the basket. This task, say Oldroyd and Wongsiri, is almost inconceivably difficult. "Imagine, if you can, sitting astride a gently swaying branch of a vast tree, high above the rest of the forest . . . in the middle of the night . . . with no safety harness and no protective clothing . . . you then reach under the branch, holding on only with your (often bare) legs to cut the comb."

There were no honey bees in the Western Hemisphere until they were brought there by the earliest European colonists. (In New England, the Indians called these strange new insects the "white man's flies.") But the native residents of the New World were by no means totally deprived of sweets. In the northeastern United States and adjoining southern Canada there was, of course, maple sugar. (The Indians taught the colonists how to make popcorn balls by mixing popped corn with sticky maple syrup.) In the Southwest, there was also honey made by wasps and ants; we will come to them later. But in Central and South America there are other kinds of bees that provide honey and wax, the stingless bees, mainly of the genera *Melipona* and *Trigona,* which are distantly related to the more familiar honey bees of the genus *Apis.* There are, as Eva Crane tells us, about five hundred species of these stingless bees in the world. They are found only in the tropics except on the high mountains and in the deserts. The great majority of these bees—about 80 percent of the species—occur only in the New World. The others are scattered in sub-Saharan Africa, Asia, the East Indies, New Guinea, and Australia.

The many species of stingless bees differ from one another in some significant ways, but they also have much in common. As Charles Michener explains, they are all highly social, and, like the honey bees, live in permanent colonies that include a queen and workers, in some species many thousands of the latter. All are said to be stingless, although they actually have a vestigial, nonfunctional stinger. Some species, reports William Morton Wheeler, a renowned early-twentieth-century ant authority, are quite docile and do little or nothing to defend their nests, while others are ferocious. As E. O. Wilson writes, some species are quick to attack intruders, including people: "They swarm over the body, pinching the skin and pulling hair, occasionally locking their mandibles in catatonic spasms so that before the grip can be broken, their heads tear loose from the body." Wilson points out that a group of species in tropical America "also eject a burning liquid from their mandibles, which in Brazil has earned them the name of *cagafogos,* meaning 'fire defecators.'"

All stingless bees forage for nectar, honeydew, and pollen except for the few species of one genus of stingless robber bees that occur in both Africa and America, which raid the nests of other bees for food. Except for one West African species, the stingless honey bees all nest in cavities, most in the hollow branches or trunks of trees, but some, reports Michener, nest in the soil, moving into the abandoned nests of ants, termites, or subterranean rodents. Their principal building material is cerumen, a mixture of propolis and wax. The bees secrete the wax but collect resins and other sticky plant substances to make propolis. Honey and pollen are stored in pots made of cerumen, which are usually egg-shaped and in the larger species may be somewhat more than 2 inches long and somewhat less than 2 inches wide. Larvae are raised in smaller tubular cells also made of cerumen.

In the tropics of most of the Eastern Hemisphere, stingless bees have been of minor importance to people, because they yield far less honey than do the native honey bees. As in the New World tropics, however, there were no honey bees in Australia and Oceania until they were introduced by Europeans. The Australian Aborigines, Crane tells us, collected honey from the nests of wild stingless bees. The yields were sometimes considerable. Varying with the species, a nest may contain no more than a mouthful of honey, or about 5 pounds, or, rarely, 40 pounds or even more. Any honey that was not eaten on the spot was carried away in baskets sealed with the cerumen of these bees. The cerumen, relates Crane, was—and may still be—valued by the Aborigines as an adhesive and a medium for making small figurines or other objects of ritual significance.

Baldwin Spencer explains that the Aborigines find nests of these bees in three ways: "The simplest is that of coming by chance across a tree where the bees can be seen flying in and out of the nest. The second is more ingenious. A native will catch a bee and fasten onto its body a little speck of light, white fluff [often spider silk] and follow it up as it flies away to its hive. The third, that I often saw them using, was to place the ear on the trunk or bough of a likely-looking gum tree, when, if it contained a nest, the low hum of the bees at work could be heard."

Like the Australian Aborigines, the Indian peoples of the New World tropics collect honey from wild nests of stingless bees. But long before the Spanish conquest, people in Mexico and Central America, and to a lesser extent in South America, had learned how to domesticate stingless bees much as Europeans domesticate honey bees. There is no doubt that honey had long been highly valued by the Indians. When the Spaniards first invaded the Aztec capital, Tenochtitlán, notes Herbert Schwarz, they found that honey was on sale in the great marketplace, where every day sixty thousand people bought or sold a wide variety of goods. The Aztecs, furthermore, demanded a tribute of honey from the native communities they had conquered. For example, the people of one area south of the Aztec capital were required to deliver twenty-four hundred jars of honey to Montezuma every year.

Honey was and still is collected from wild nests throughout most of the New World tropics. According to Schwarz, some tribes pillage the nests so ruthlessly that they give the bees no opportunity to recuperate. Others treat the bees more considerately and wisely. When they find "a bees' nest in the forest, they do not utterly destroy it but leave enough of it to induce the bees to persist in their efforts at replacement, so that when they again visit the spot, they may exact another enforced contribution." This custom may well have been the first step in the domestication of stingless bees. In Bolivia, organized bands of from ten to twenty natives would, from June to September, systematically search the forest for the nests of wild stingless bees to obtain honey and cerumen. In addition to plundering and destroying the nests, they would often carry off a whole colony and domesticate it.

No stingless bee has been more often domesticated than *Melipona beecheii,* known to the Maya of the Yucatán as *colel-cab* (lady bee) or *xunan-cab* (hive bee). The domestication of stingless bees, according to Crane, reached its highest level in Central America, where the Maya lived in an organized civilization; it was less common in South America, where most of the native peoples were hunter-gatherers. The importance in the New World of beekeeping as a source of honey and wax is shown by the fact that some Mayan beekeepers kept as many as four hundred to seven hundred hives of stingless bees in historical times.

Most often the hives are made from sections 2 to 3 feet long cut from a hollow log. A small hole, the entrance and exit for the bees, is drilled at the midpoint of the section, and the ends of the section are plugged with clay or some other material. The hive is suspended horizontally from a tree or some other support. A wandering swarm may take possession of the hive, but the beekeeper usually "seeds" the hive with a cluster of brood cells accompanied by a queen and a few workers. The honey is harvested by removing the plugs from the two ends of the hive and removing the honeypots.

The honey of stingless bees, generally much more watery than that of honey bees, sooner or later ferments and sours after it has been harvested and removed from the cerumen honeypots. In Brazil, Schwarz reports, the honey of stingless bees is preserved by cooking it to evaporate water, thereby increasing the concentration of sugar, which increases the osmotic pressure that kills yeast and other living organisms in the honey.

The peoples of the New World prepare intoxicating drinks from the honey of stingless bees just as the people of the Old World make mead and other intoxicating drinks from the honey of honey bees. We read in Schwarz's book that the Indians of Paraguay "took a raw and dried hide of a jaguar or of a deer, which they suspended in such a way that it formed a pouch. Into it they dumped the honey as well as the wax, poured water upon these, and left the mixture to ferment under the heat of the sun. In three or four days the brew thus exposed attained the desired degree of potency. To designated tasters was assigned the responsibility of testing the progress of the brew and determining whether it had the right strength."

In the New World, harvesting wild honey and, even more, beekeeping have involved religious beliefs, superstitions, and rituals. In Vera Cruz, Mexico, the natives believed that the *abejas reales* (royal bees), *Melipona beecheii,* which happen to be the most productive of the stingless bees, will desert their nest if certain rules and rituals are not observed. The bees are particularly offended by domestic squabbles. Therefore, the Indians believe that a man who has two or more wives is not likely to be a successful beekeeper. This is similar to the Central European superstition that honey bees will not thrive if their owner's family is quarrelsome or if one member of the family deceives another. Indians of some tribes believe that they must practice sexual abstinence for seven nights before opening a hive. At the end of this period, the beekeeper goes out before sunrise and smokes the hive with copal (resin from various trees) before removing the honey. Similarly, sexual abstinence was required of beekeepers and their assistants by a tribe in Kenya.

You would hardly expect colonial wasps to make honey, because all species of colonial wasps are predators, diligent hunters that capture caterpillars and other insects to feed to the colony's larval offspring as do the familiar North American species such as the yellow jacket and the bald-faced hornet. Nevertheless, there are a very few mostly tropical species that make honey in addition to preying on insects. These species not only make honey but store such large quantities of it that in some places they are harvested by people. But what do the wasps themselves use this honey for? Not much is known about this, but Howard Evans and Mary Jane West Eberhard speculate that they probably feed it to larvae. At a 1905 meeting of the Entomological Society of Washington, a Mr. Barber

> exhibited an original photograph of a wasp nest from Brownsville, Texas, made by *Nectarina mellifica* Say. He was told by the Negro who had possession of the nest that these wasps produce a palatable honey and that it is customary for the Mexicans to secure the nests when small and keep them until of full size, then destroying the wasps and extracting the honey. The

> nest was similar to those of our common paper-making wasp [the bald-faced hornet]... except that in its lower portion the cells were exposed. It was globular in shape and about nine inches in diameter—not of full size, according to the Negro, who, after cautiously inserting a knife into it, withdrawing it and examining the blade, asserted that there was yet too little honey contents to make it worth while to open it up.

This wasp, according to J. Philip Spradbery, forms huge colonies that may include ten thousand to fifteen thousand individuals and may persist for several years. According to Wilson, in South America colonies of a related species may persist for as long as twenty-five years.

For reasons that we don't need to discuss, taxonomists (experts on the naming and classification of organisms) have changed the generic name of this wasp from *Nectarina* to *Brachygastra*. *Nectarina mellifica* can be roughly translated from Latin as "the nectar collector that makes honey." The Latin root of the specific name appears in the English word *mellifluous*. A mellifluous voice is as smooth as honey. *Brachygastra* is descriptive of the adult wasp—it means "short abdomen" in Greek—but it is not nearly as appealing or mellifluous a name as *Nectarina mellifica*.

Evans and Eberhard described the commercial exploitation of the honey of one of the seven species of this genus known at the time they wrote:

> In Brazil the honey of *Brachygastra lecheguana* is gathered from large nests, usually during the Brazilian summer. If the base of the nest is left on the branch the inhabitants rebuild it in the same place, and the colony can be exploited again the next year. In Mexico the honey of *B. lecheguana* has commercial value. Wasp farmers gather young nests and transplant them to places where they can be protected, then periodically oust the inhabitants from the nest with smoke, destroy the nest to obtain the honey, and allow the wasps to return and rebuild the colony.... Consumers of wasp honey are

> well-advised to patronize a trustworthy vespiculturist [wasp keeper], for the honey of *B. lecheguana* is occasionally poisonous because of the incorporation of nectar from certain flowers.

Like bees, these wasps collect the nectar of a wide variety of flowering plants and also, as Evans and Eberhard note, any available source of concentrated sugar, including manmade sweets, ripe fruits, and the honeydew (sugary excrement) of sap-sucking insects such as aphids and treehoppers. They even steal honey stored by bees.

Treehoppers, leafhoppers, aphids, and related insects use their piercing-sucking beaks to feed on the plant's phloem sap, which transports sugar and various other nutrients from the leaves, where they are synthesized, down to the roots, where they are stored. Because it is under pressure, phloem sap is actually forced up into the insect's beak. J. S. Kennedy and T. E. Mittler found that if a feeding aphid is snipped from the plant, leaving its beak still embedded in the phloem tube, sap continues to flow from the severed beak even though the sucking organs have been removed. (This entomological discovery enabled plant physiologists for the first time to easily obtain pure phloem sap, the chemical composition of which was a central problem in their field.) Phloem sap, which is mostly water, is very rich in sugars but low in other nutrients. Consequently, in order to acquire enough of these other nutrients, such as protein and vitamins, aphids, treehoppers, and other phloem feeders imbibe more than enough water and usually an excess of sugars, which they discard in their excrement, which is consequently little more than a solution of sugars in water—hence the name *honeydew.* Many of these insects secrete several times their body weight of honeydew each day.

Honeydew is collected by honey bees, which incorporate it into their

honey. Consequently, many of us have consumed honeydew indirectly. For example, my friend and colleague Gene Robinson informs me that the Germans particularly prize honey made from honeydew that bees collect from fir trees in the Black Forest. But in some parts of the world, people relish honeydew that they themselves collect from plants. The Aborigines of Australia, according to Friedrich Bodenheimer, collect large quantities of the honeydew so abundantly excreted by jumping plant lice (family Psyllidae) on acacia trees. These insects look like tiny cicadas but are really much like aphids except that they have jumping hind legs and both sexes are always winged in the adult stage. In Central Australia, almost every leaf of some red gums, a species of eucalyptus, is covered with large colonies of jumping plant lice that produce surprisingly large amounts of honeydew, referred to as "lerp-manna" by Bodenheimer, and as *prelja* by the native Arunta people. In season, the natives collect large quantities of this sweet.

The Kurds of western Turkey and northern Iraq are famous throughout the Middle East for the delicious confection they make from honeydew excreted by aphids that live on oaks. The Kurds cut branches from oaks early

Above: Stroked by an ant's antennae, an aphid exudes a drop of honeydew.

in the morning before ants have appropriated the honeydew for themselves. Then the branches are beaten to knock off the honeydew, which is often quite abundant. In the region's dry air, it soon hardens into a rocklike mass, which is sold to confectioners, who dissolve it in water and strain it through a cloth to remove aphids and debris such as leaf fragments. The filtered honeydew is mixed with seasonings, almonds, and eggs and then boiled and allowed to cool and solidify. It is ready to eat after being cut into pieces and coated with powdered sugar. An Iraqi acquaintance told me that it is delicious and that, once tasted, its flavor is never forgotten. Honeydew is called *man* in Hebrew. In Arabic it is also called *man,* and *man-es-simma* means "honeydew that falls from the sky." Some entomologists believe that honeydew produced by scale insects that live on tamarind trees is the manna that miraculously fell from heaven to nourish the ancient Israelites as they fled across the Sinai desert from Egypt. Exodus 16:31 says of this honeydew, "And the house of Israel called the name thereof Manna: and it was like coriander seed, white; and the taste of it was like wafers made with honey."

In *The Naturalist in Nicaragua,* Thomas Belt gives an account of a *Brachygastra* wasp that was collecting honeydew from an aggregation of treehoppers and was constantly skirmishing with ants that were collecting honeydew from the same insects:

> The wasp stroked the young hoppers, and sipped up the honey when it was exuded, just like the ants. When an ant came up to a cluster of leaf-hoppers [*sic*] attended by a wasp, the latter would not attempt to grapple with its rival on the leaf, but would fly off and hover over the ant; then when its little foe was well exposed, it would dart at it and strike it to the ground. The action was so quick that I could not determine whether it struck with its fore-feet or its jaws, but I think it was with the feet. I often saw a wasp trying to clear a leaf from ants that were already in full possession of a cluster of leaf-hoppers.

> It would sometimes have to strike three or four times at an ant before it made it quit its hold and fall. At other times one ant after the other would be struck off with great celerity and ease, and I fancied that some wasps were much cleverer than others.

Ants of a number of species, but most likely not those that Belt observed, store honey for future consumption. In common parlance they are known as the honeypot ants. Unlike the bees and wasps that we just met, they do not fabricate combs or pots made of wax or paper for honey storage. They evolved their own amazing and unique storage system. Some of the worker ants of a colony serve as honeypots, living vessels for the long-term storage of honey. They are ready and waiting as other workers are out foraging. When the foragers return with their crops loaded with nectar or honeydew, they regurgitate their bounty to the honeypots, whose abdomens, as Wilson puts it, become "so distended that they have difficulty moving and are forced to remain permanently in the nest as 'living honey casks.'" Fully loaded honeypot workers—no fewer than fifteen hundred in an underground nest in Arizona—hang from the ceiling by their legs until their stores are required.

Honeypot ants of different species are found—mainly in hot, arid areas—in the southwestern United States, Mexico, Australia, New Guinea, and New Caledonia. The laboratory studies of Robert Stumper suggest how long-term honey storage fosters the survival of these ants in their inhospitable desert habitats. When Stumper held ants at a cool 68°F, they seldom tapped into their store of honey but continually and diligently added to it; at 86°F, however, the ants drew on their honey stores. It seems that when conditions are favorable, cool and moist, little of the stored honey is eaten, but when it is hot and dry and nectar is scarce, the metabolic rate of the ants is high and they survive by drawing on their store of energy-rich honey. As

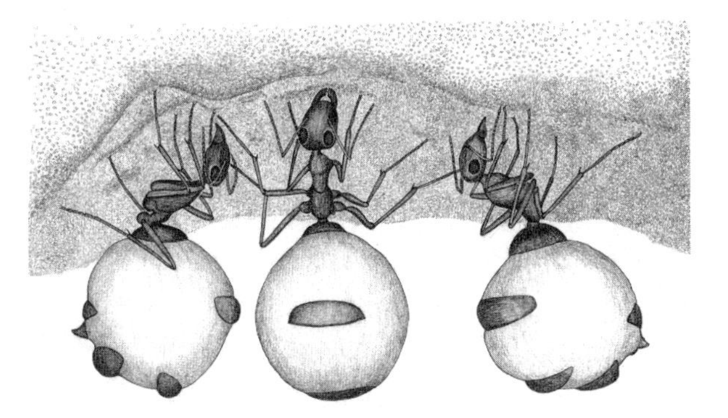

long ago as 1882, H. C. McCook, cited by Friedrich Bodenheimer, reported that "after proper titillating" by other ants, honeypots "are induced in times of scarcity to regurgitate their honey."

The original inhabitants of Australia, Mexico, and the western United States gathered honeypot ants, and to some extent still do, as a small but important and much relished sweet addition to their diet. In 1908, William Morton Wheeler quoted from an 1832 publication by Pablo de Llave, who related that in Mexico

> the peasant women and children are well acquainted with these nests, that they seek them assiduously for the purpose of obtaining the honey and that when they are going to make a present of them, they take hold of them very cautiously, carefully remove the head and thorax and then place them in a dish; but if the insects are to be eaten as soon as found, the saccharine portion is sucked out and the remainder thrown away. The head and thorax are removed, I was told, to prevent the ants from injuring one another,

Above: Worker ants serving as honeypots hang from the ceiling of a chamber in an underground nest.

> for although they are unable to walk, owing to the prodigious volume of the abdomen, they nevertheless struggle when placed in a dish, and catch hold of and rupture one another, so that in the end they become flaccid and depleted. Indeed, the skin which unites the segments of the abdomen is so delicate and especially so distended, on account of the enormous quantity of honey which it contains, that the least puncture causes the contents to flow out.

In an 1875 article by W. Saunders in the *Canadian Entomologist,* we read that in New Mexico "the natives make a very pleasant drink from the honey of a honeypot ant. In Mexico, women and children dig them up and enjoy their honey, and it is by no means unusual for these insects to be served at table, the head and thorax with the legs being removed, when the distended abdomens are eaten as a delicate sweetmeat."

In *Insects as Human Food,* Friedrich Bodenheimer, relying on the reports of several observers, informs us that in the interior deserts of Australia, "honey ants" are important food for the Aborigines and are one of the few sweets available to them. So important is the honeypot ant to these people that it is the totem of one of the clans of the Arunta tribe. While the women and children stand by quietly, the men—their bodies smeared all over with dry ochre and decorated with twigs of the *udnirringa* bush—conduct long and elaborate honeypot ceremonies. But the women of the tribe do all the work of foraging for honeypots. They locate nests by looking for the openings of the burrows, which are not accompanied by a mound of earth and are the only—and difficult to find—outward sign of a nest. Working with surprising speed, a woman loosens the hard soil around the burrow with her digging stick and throws it over her shoulder with her bare hand or a small dish. In some places, the "whole surface of the ground has been turned up, just as if a small army of prospectors had been at work." She follows the main burrow, which goes down as much as 6 feet. A few honeypots are found in horizontal burrows that go off in all directions from the vertical burrow, but most are in a large chamber at the bottom of the nest.

"When a native wishes to partake of the honey, he grips one of the ants by the head, and placing the swollen abdomen between his lips he squeezes the contents into his mouth," Bodenheimer writes. He says of the honeypot's flavor that the palate first "receives a prick of formic acid," the ant's chemical defense. "But this is slight and momentary; and the instant the membrane bursts, it is followed by a delicious and rich flavor of honey."

Insects, as you will see next, have been used both rationally and superstitiously as cures and palliatives for almost any human ailment that you can think of. The use of some of these medicinal insects is effective and is still practiced in modern times. Many other "cures" are worthless, however—nothing more than superstitions born of ignorance. Some of these are even, from a modern point of view, hilarious.

IX Cures and Nostrums

When William Beebe excavated an underground nest of leaf-cutter ants in 1921 in British Guiana (now the nation Guyana), he was attacked by a horde of the furiously defensive ants. Among them were tiny workers, others of medium size, and gigantic soldiers almost an inch long with huge, powerful mandibles that they viciously and firmly sank into the leather of his boots. When he unpacked these boots the following year, he "found the heads and jaws of two [of the soldiers] still firmly attached, relics of some forgotten foray of the preceding year." He went on to say, "This mechanical vise-like grip, wholly independent of life or death, is utilized by the Guiana Indians. In place of stitching up extensive wounds, a number of these giant [leaf-cutter soldiers] are collected and their jaws applied to the edges of the skin, which are drawn together. The ants take hold, their bodies are snipped off, and the row of jaws remains until the wound is healed."

Across the sea in the Eastern Hemisphere, E.W. Gudger relates, the innovative use of ants as sutures to close wounds began in India before 2000 B.C.E. This practice was first described in the fourth division of the Vedas, the ancient Sanskrit books of knowledge, which are the oldest literary monument of Indian medicine. Living black ants were used to close incisions in "the walls of the intestines, during the operation for intestinal obstruction." And this more than three thousand years ago! This knowledge was later acquired by the Arabs who, in the name of Islam, swept out of Arabia in the eighth century C.E. to conquer all of northern Africa and Spain, and some of southern France. Albucasis, an Arabian physician who practiced in Spain in the twelfth century, used ants to suture wounds. In late medieval and early Renaissance times in Europe, ants were widely used to close wounds. Several surgeons at the time derided this use of ants, which they thought to be long outmoded, and the practice seems to have been discontinued by European surgeons sometime after the seventeenth century. It survived at least until the end of the nineteenth century, however, in the eastern and southern Mediterranean areas.

In about 1890, according to Gudger, a gentleman's forehead was cut when he fell from his horse in Asian Turkey. As was the custom of the country, he went to a Greek barber to have the wound treated:

> Pressing together the margins of the cut with the fingers of the left hand, [the barber] applied the insect by means of a pair of forceps held in the right hand. The mandibles of the ant were widely open for self-defense, and as the insect was carefully brought near to the wound, it seized upon the raised surface, penetrated the skin on both sides, and remained tenaciously fixed while the operator severed the head from the thorax, so leaving the mandibles grasping the wound. The same operation was repeated until about ten ants' heads were fixed on the wound, and left in position for three days or thereabouts, when the cut was healed and the heads removed.

In 1945, a French surgeon, whose words were translated by Gudger, reported that in Algeria a beetle was used to suture wounds much as the ant was. This insect, of the genus *Scarites,* is a ground beetle (family Carabidae) with unusually long and sharply pointed mandibles. After a beetle had bitten together the edges of the wound, its body was separated from the head. The Algerian doctors covered the base of the mandibles with an adhesive in order to keep them from separating, but the French surgeon said that this was an unnecessary precaution, because the mandibles were so tightly locked that they would have to be broken to get rid of the head. Using ants or beetles as clamps is surely faster and more convenient than sewing up a wound and tying numerous knots. When I recently had an operation to mend a broken wrist, the surgeon closed the incision with metal staples, clamps that work just like the mandibles of ants or beetles.

There is no doubt that the ant mandibles work very well. But we now tend to view *all* such "folk remedies" as unsophisticated or nothing more than superstitions. Our attitude may well date back to a backlash against the fallacious medieval doctrine of signatures, which held that every plant or animal on Earth was put here by the Creator to serve humans, and that He marked each with a "signature" that indicates to what use it can be put. Hence, the plant known as the liverwort was, with more faith than reason, assumed to cure liver problems because its leaves are shaped like a liver. An insect with an ear-shaped hind wing, the earwig, was imagined to be a cure for earaches. But by no means are all folk remedies useless. As you will see, honey has real medicinal properties. A decoction of willow bark is an ancient folk remedy for headaches and fever. Willow contains aspirin, salicylic acid, its technical chemical name, which is derived from the generic name of the willows, *Salix.* The most familiar astringent today is the alum (an aluminum compound) in the styptic pencils used in shaving to stop nicks from bleeding, but, according to Frank Cowan, tannins from galls, such as those used in making ink,

"are the most powerful of all the vegetable astringents" and were used with success in the nineteenth century. Further evidence of the efficacy of some folk remedies is the many successes of the modern pharmaceutical scouts who have traveled the world to pick the brains of tribal shamans (medicine men) in the often realized hope of gaining knowledge of folk remedies that may yield new and effective drugs.

Many folk remedies—once used with naïve confidence—are patently worthless, however, and are likely to be amusing from our more sophisticated point of view. For example, according to Cowan, "the Lady-bird [beetle] was formerly considered an efficacious remedy for the colic and measles; and it has been recommended often as a cure for the toothache: being said,

---

Above: According to the doctrine of signatures, the earlike shape of this earwig's hind wing indicates that it will cure earaches.

when one or two are mashed and put into the hollow tooth, to immediately relieve the pain." He also tells us:

> In the latter part of the eighteenth century, there was published at Florence, by Prof. Gergi, the history of a remarkable insect [a snout beetle, a weevil] which he names *Curculio anti-odontalgicus.* This insect, as he assures us, not only in the name he has given it, but also in an account of the many cures effected by it, is endowed with the singular property of curing the toothache. He tells us, that if fourteen or fifteen of the larvae be rubbed between the thumb and fore-finger, till the fluid is absorbed, and if a carious aching tooth be but touched with the thumb or finger thus prepared, the pain will be removed; a finger thus prepared, he says in conclusion, will, unless it be used for tooth-touching, retain its virtue for a year!

It was also believed that deafness could be cured by putting into the ear a pulverized earwig mixed with the urine of a hare. Pliny the Elder advised that an earache could be alleviated by placing in the ear a wad of wool soaked with rose oil containing the pulverized remains of a fatty beetle; however, he warned, the wool must soon be withdrawn lest it give rise to a "grub or little worme." According to J. G. Wood's 1883 *Insects at Home,* Swedish peasants believed that the bite of a grasshopper would cause warts to disappear. It was said that bedbugs neutralize the venom of snakes. Cowan tells us that the least revolting way of using these blood-sucking insects was to crush them and apply them externally with the blood of a tortoise. He also reports that powdered dry silkworms were thought to "remove vertigos and convulsions" if applied to the crown of the head. Pliny the Elder wrote that if a stag beetle is "tied about the necks of children, it enables them to retain their urine," and that "the galls of the field cirsium [a thistle] formerly enjoyed a very great reputation, for it was considered, when carried simply in the pocket, as a sovereign remedy against hemorrhages." Cowan informs us that a Roman consul "carried about him a living Fly... wrapped in a piece of white linen, and strongly asserted that to the use of this expedient he owed his preservation from ophthalmia." Cowan also quotes what is, from the modern point of view, an exceptionally amusing cure for baldness:

> "Varro affirmeth," says Pliny, "that the heads of Flies applied fresh to the bald place, is a convenient medicine for the said infirmity and defect. Some use in this case the blood of flies: others mingle their ashes with the ashes of paper used in old time, or els of nuts; with this proportion, that there be a third part only of the ashes of flies to the rest, and herewith for ten days together rubb the bare places where the hair is gone. Some there be againe, who temper and incorporate together the said ashes of Flies with the juice of colewort and brest-milke: others take nothing thereto but honey."

The so-called Spanish fly, a blister beetle (family Meloidae), secretes cantharidin, an irritating chemical that causes the skin to blister, and that was once, given by mouth, futilely and dangerously used as an aphrodisiac. And in days gone by, physicians applied it to the skin for its irritating and warming effect, much as your great-grandmother may have applied an irritating mustard plaster to her child's chest in the mistaken belief that it would ease the symptoms of a cold. Robert L. Metcalf and Robert A. Metcalf quote an author who wrote, "The barbarisms practiced on the American people during the nineteenth century by the application of cantharis blisters for all sorts of ailments, overtopped the misery endured by those who suffered in the war of the Revolution."

Nevertheless, as you will see, certain insects and insect products are actually useful and respectable remedies in use today to alleviate human ailments.

Scavenging insects such as the maggots (larvae) of the black, bluebottle, and greenbottle blow flies perform an indispensable ecological service by recycling the bodies of dead animals. One of their close relatives, the disreputable and infamous screwworm fly, infests wounds on living animals such as cows and even people and feeds on healthy, living flesh; but the blow flies eat only dead flesh. For this reason, the maggots of blow flies, notably the greenbottle fly (*Lucilia sericata*) and the black blow fly (*Phormia regina*), are very useful in the practice of medicine for debriding, removing dead flesh from wounds.

In 1931, William Baer, an army physician who had served during the First World War, wrote of his experiences treating wounded soldiers in Europe:

> At a certain battle during 1917, two soldiers with compound fractures of the femur and large flesh wounds of the abdomen and scrotum were brought into the hospital. These men had been wounded during an engagement and in such a part of the country, hidden by brush, that when the wounded of that battle were picked up they were overlooked. For seven days they lay on the battlefield without water, without food, and exposed to the weather and all the insects which were about that region. On their arrival at the hospital I found that they had no fever and that there was no evidence of septicaemia or blood poisoning....
>
> This unusual fact quickly attracted my attention. I could not understand how a man who had lain on the ground for seven days with a compound fracture of the femur, without food and water, should be free of fever and of evidences of sepsis. On removing the clothing from the wounded part, much was my surprise to see the wound filled with thousands and thousands of maggots, apparently those of the blow fly....
>
> The sight was very disgusting and measures were taken hurriedly to wash out these abominable looking creatures. Then the wounds were irrigated with normal salt solution and the most remarkable picture was presented in

> the character of the wound which was exposed. Instead of having a wound filled with pus, as one would have expected, due to the degeneration of devitalized tissue and to the presence of the numerous types of bacteria, these wounds were filled with the most beautiful pink granulation tissue that one could imagine. [Granulation is a step in the process of healing.]

Baer went on to use maggots as debriding agents in what is now known as "maggot therapy."

Baer had expressed a common human prejudice by referring to the maggots as "abominable looking creatures." Persuaded by the evidence before his eyes, however, he soon overcame this unreasonable prejudice and published the scholarly article quoted above, on the treatment of infected wounds with maggots. (Maggot therapy is also known by names that may be less disturbing to squeamish patients: larval therapy and biodebridement.)

Baer's discovery was not new. Maggot therapy, according to Ronald Sherman and Edward Pechter, was used by the ancient Mayan people of Mexico and Guatemala, in Australia by the Ngemba tribe of New South Wales, and by the hill people of Burma (now Myanmar). In 1829, a surgeon in Napoleon's army discovered that maggots in battle wounds prevented infection and promoted healing. But it is not known if he applied his new knowledge and practiced maggot therapy. A Confederate surgeon, noted Baer, may well have been the first Western doctor to actually use maggot therapy. He reported that the maggots would, in only one day, clean a wound much better than any other agents or methods that he had at his command. He believed that his use of maggots saved the limbs or lives of a number of wounded soldiers.

By Baer's time, according to Sherman and his coauthors, maggot therapy had become an accepted medical technique. About one thousand American surgeons used it, and the Lederle Corporation sold sterile maggots for five dollars per thousand (equivalent to one hundred current dollars). Before 1933, according to William Robinson, maggot therapy was used in three hundred hospitals in the United States and Canada, and some hospitals had their own facilities for rearing sterile maggots.

When sulfa drugs and antibiotics such as penicillin became available, the use of maggots dwindled. By the mid-1940s they were seldom used, and then only as a last resort. In 1990, for example, a Champaign, Illinois, surgeon used blow fly maggots to cure an otherwise intractable, chronic, deep-seated infection in the leg of a diabetic woman, saving her from having her leg amputated. As the surgeon's nurse told me, "When all conventional methods fail, you do what you have to do." In past years, University of Illinois entomologists have on several occasions supplied sterile maggots to local physicians.

During recent years the use of medicinal maggots has been steadily increasing owing to the ever-expanding resistance of pathogenic bacteria to antibiotics, accelerated by the unthinking overuse of antibiotics. The number of resistant bacterial species is constantly growing. Some, such as the *Staphylococcus* so often present in hospitals, have become resistant to almost all currently available antibiotics. In the year 2000, Sherman observed that "worldwide the number of practitioners or centres employing this therapy has increased from less than a dozen in 1995, to almost 1,000 today." He reported that in the United Kingdom from 1995 to 2000, ten thousand batches of sterile maggots were sent to seven hundred treatment centers. In 2004, according to the science writer Barbara Maynard, Sherman "sent out 1,500 vials of maggots to physicians and clinics in the United States, and more than 30,000 vials worldwide."

At first glance it would seem to be a difficult problem to sterilize maggots. This is true of flesh flies (family Sarcophagidae) because they give birth to

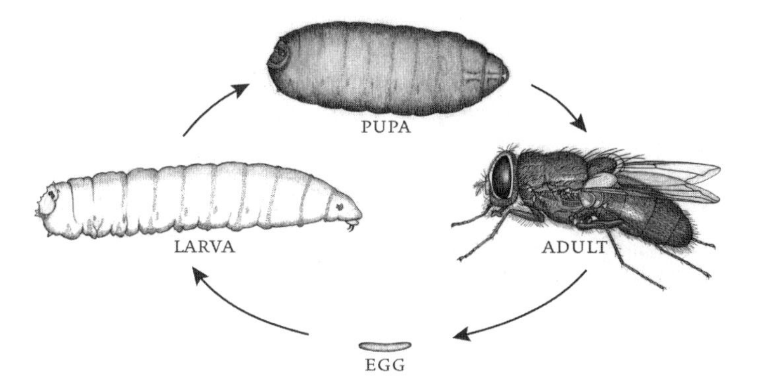

tiny living larvae rather than laying eggs as do the blow flies (family Calliphoridae). Tiny newly born flesh fly maggots are delicate and difficult to sterilize without harming them. The larvae of blow flies are protected by the shells of the eggs, however, and the eggs can be safely sterilized with chemical disinfectant without harming the embryos within them.

Just exactly what do maggots do to heal an infected wound? They do what surgeons do—but with more finesse and much more sparingly—when they debride wounds. *Debridement* is defined by *Webster's New Collegiate Dictionary* as "the surgical removal of lacerated, devitalized, or contaminated [infected] tissue." When a surgeon cuts away dead tissue with a scalpel, he or she cannot help but remove some healthy tissue. Maggots, on the other hand, remove dead tissue virtually cell by cell, and being very fussy feeders, remove and eat only dead cells—never healthy ones. When the maggots are full-grown, they leave the wound and are removed from the dressing. In nature, they—like almost all fly larvae—leave the site where they have fed, most often on a dead animal but occasionally in a festering wound on a liv-

---

Above: The maggot, or larva, shown in this life cycle of the blow fly is used in maggot therapy.

ing animal, to descend to the soil, where they make a shallow burrow and metamorphose to the pupal stage.

In addition to removing dead tissue, maggots also facilitate and hasten the healing of wounds and disinfect them. There is growing evidence that certain substances produced by maggots hasten healing by promoting the growth of granulation tissue. As long ago as 1935, William Robinson found that maggots stimulate healing by flooding the wound with allantoin, a waste product of the metabolism of proteins that has antibiotic properties. The secretion of this antibiotic substance serves the maggots well, for their main competitors for dead tissue are bacteria.

Not only is honey a delicious and nutritious sweet, but over the centuries—really millennia—many authors of various cultures have written of its medicinal properties, some only imagined but others demonstrably efficacious. In recent years there has been, as we will see, a resurgence of interest in honey's healing qualities.

In an article titled "The First Pharmacopeia in Man's Recorded History," Samuel Kramer discusses a Sumerian clay tablet inscribed with cuneiform script that records the recipe for what is presumably a poultice: "Pulverize river clay, knead it with water and honey; let 'sea' oil and hot cedar oil be spread over it." The tablet, about four thousand years old, was found in the ruins of the city of Nippur, which is not far from modern Baghdad and was the spiritual and cultural center of the ancient Sumerian civilization. A thirty-five-hundred-year-old papyrus manuscript from ancient Egypt, writes Eva Crane, includes 147 prescriptions containing honey and intended for external use. According to Guido Majno, in ancient Egyptian papyri honey is listed as an ingredient in five hundred out of nine hundred medicines. Other papyri recommend honey as a component of "dressings for wounds, burns, abscesses, and suppurating sores, skin conditions due to scurvy." A mixture of crocodile feces, honey, and saltpeter was prescribed as a contraceptive. In 1993, Crane was told by Egyptians that cotton soaked in honey and lemon juice was then still used as a contraceptive.

The ancient Greeks and Romans, like the Egyptians, valued not only honey but also beeswax and propolis for their real or presumed medicinal properties. (Propolis, as you have seen, is a sticky substance that consists of plant resins collected by honey bees.) Hilda Ransome notes that Dioscorides, the great Greek physician, pharmacologist, and author of *De materia medica,* written in 90 C.E., often mentioned honey, honey wines, beeswax, and propolis as medicines. Although Dioscorides was a Greek, he accompanied the armies of the Roman emperor Nero as a surgeon. Written in Greek but soon translated into Latin and eventually into several other languages, his *De materia medica* was the medical "bible" of the ancient Mediterranean civilizations, and in Europe was the primary text of pharmacology until the end of the fifteenth century. It was written in five books. The second considers the medicinal and dietetic values of animal products and derivatives such as honey, propolis, and beeswax.

Written almost six hundred years after Dioscorides' book, the Koran, the holy book of the Muslims, says of the honey bee (in the English translation by N.J. Dawood): "From its belly comes forth a syrup of different hues, a cure for men. Surely in this there is a sign for those who would take thought (Surah 16:68)." In 1371 C.E., Kam al nil-Din ad-Amiri, in what Ransome refers to as a curious book on animals, wrote: "The best honey is in the comb, and it is excellent as a medicine, but if it is cooked in water it loses its healing properties. It is especially good for the eyes, and it is good to give a dog if bitten by another."

For centuries honey has been used as a medicine in mainland Europe and the British Isles. For example, the medicinal value of honey was recognized in pre-Christian Finland. We read in Ransome's *The Sacred Bee* a quotation from the *Kalevala,* a group of Finnish legends transmitted orally until put into print in the nineteenth century:

> From the earth the bee rose swiftly,
> On his honeyed wings rose whirring,
> And he soared on rapid pinions,
> Swiftly past the moon he hurried,
> Past the borders of the sunlight,
> Rose upon the Great Bear's shoulders,
> O'er the Seven Stars' backs rose upwards,
> Flew to the Creator's cellars,
> To the halls of the Almighty;
> There the drugs were well concocted,
> And the ointment duly tempered
> In the pots composed of silver,
> Or within the golden kettles.

This was the honey ointment a mother needed to bring her son back to life:

> Tis the ointment that I needed,
> And the salve of the Almighty,
> Used when Jumala the Highest,
> The Creator heals all suffering.

Jumala, also known as Ukko, is the pagan god of the sky.

The first book on honey in English, written by John Hill in 1759, and cited by R. B. Willson and Eva Crane, was *The Virtue of Honey in Preventing Many of the Worst Disorders; and in the Certain Cure of Several Others; Particularly the Gravel, Asthmas, Coughs, Hoarseness, and a Tough Morning Phlegm.* It should be noted that to this day honey is often an ingredient of cough drops.

An old Irish folktale cited by Ransome tells of an Irishman who became ill. His hair turned white and he soon became nothing but skin and bones. It concludes with the advice given to him by a beggar: "'You must go to the bees and fetch so much honey that you can rub yourself all over with it from head to foot. But you must fetch the honey yourself, if anyone does it for you, it won't do you any good. The bees fly to all the flowers, suck the goodness out of them and mix this in their honey. It will cure you, make your hair brown again, and your face fresh and red.' The Irishman followed this advice and was soon as well as ever."

Our language reflects the ancient association of honey with medicine. As Charles Hogue points out, "The word 'medicine' owes its origin to honey; the first syllable has the same root as mead," the honey wine that you learned of in chapter 8, which was often "consumed as an elixir." Metheglin is mead spiced with cloves, ginger, rosemary, thyme, or other herbs. Its name derives from the Welsh word for physician, *meddyglyn,* reflecting metheglin's reputed medicinal powers.

Although honey has been credited with curative powers that are often obviously ridiculous—at least from our modern point of view—it does have real medicinal properties that are suggested by a great deal of anecdotal evidence and are in some instances demonstrated by scientific data. For example, in *Honey, the Gourmet Medicine,* Joe Traynor relates the following anecdote: A registered nurse burned her arm and applied a commercial burn ointment. Several days later, she suffered a similar burn on the other arm and treated it with honey. A few days later, "the honey-treated arm was completely healed; the ointment-treated burn was still evident."

In 1998, M. Subrahmanyam, a physician, published convincing scientific evidence of the effectiveness of honey as a treatment for burns. He had previously published in medical journals five other research articles that demonstrated the effectiveness of honey in healing the injury caused by burns that is visible to the naked eye. In his 1998 article, he went a step farther by taking biopsies of burned tissue before and after treatment to show the effects of healing at the microscopic, cellular level. By comparing two groups of twenty-five randomly selected burn victims treated with either honey or the usual silver sulfadiazine cream, he showed that by the seventh day of treatment 84 percent of the honey-treated group, but only 72 percent of the silver sulfadiazine–treated group, showed visible signs of healing. By the twenty-first day all of the honey-treated burns, but only 84 percent of the silver sulfadiazine group, were healing. These results were supported by microscopic examination of the biopsied tissue. Eighty percent and 100 percent of the biopsies of honey-treated burns showed signs of tissue repair on the seventh and twenty-first days, respectively, whereas in the sulfadiazine-treated group the corresponding percentages were 52 and 84. Subrahmanyam's results show that honey is *at least* as effective as the conventional silver sulfadiazine treatment and probably significantly *more* effective.

There is also considerable anecdotal and some scientific evidence that honey alleviates or even cures other illnesses, including stomach ulcers, irritable bowel syndrome, some forms of cancer, liver problems, cataracts and other eye disorders, coughs, tooth decay, hangovers, and even bad hair days. The last two "maladies" on this list probably made you chuckle. Traynor, however, is serious. The sugar and enzyme content of honey hastens the metabolism of alcohol and thereby "gives quicker recovery from overindulgence." A mixture of honey and olive oil is a good hair conditioner if worked into the hair before shampooing. On a more serious note, there is not only anecdotal but also scientific evidence that honey can cure stomach ulcers, which are now known to be caused primarily by bacteria; irritable bowel syndrome caused by bacterial gastroenteritis; and various ailments of the eyes. Some of the anecdotal evidence is quite compelling although it is not rigorous scientific "proof." For example, Traynor writes that a man suffering from severe, possibly terminal stomach ulcers hated doctors, so he stayed at home and suffered. A friend told him about a Russian study showing that honey cured ulcers. The man embarked on a honey diet—honey and freshly squeezed grapefruit juice, nothing else—and was "miraculously" cured.

But how does honey effect these cures? Bacteria and other microorganisms cannot live and grow in honey. As you read in chapter 8, honey contains such a high concentration of sugars and so little water that the much larger amount of water in a bacterium, or any other organism, diffuses into the honey by osmosis. Desiccation, the loss of water, kills the bacterium.

Honey also contains various antibacterial substances derived from the nectar that bees collect and convert into honey. This is to be expected because plants produce a great variety of substances that protect them, not only against plant-eating insects, but also against bacteria and fungi. Because different plants contain different protective substances, the nature and concentration of them in honey varies with the species of plant from which the bees collected nectar. For example, a dark honey derived from the nectar of the manuka plant, a small flowering shrub found in New Zealand, has more medicinal value than most other honeys, and, generally speaking, dark-colored honeys, such as those made from nectar collected from buckwheat flowers, have more medicinal value than light-colored honeys.

Manuka honeys are not all equally effective as antibacterials. In New Zealand, the antibacterial potency of the different varieties is measured and compared with the potency of the antiseptic phenol (carbolic acid). The result is the UMF (unique manuka factor) of the honey. A UMF of ten is equivalent to the potency of a 10 percent solution of carbolic acid. According to Traynor, a 17-ounce jar of manuka honey with a UMF of ten or better sells for $25, while a 17-ounce jar of unrated manuka honey costs only $3.39 (2001 prices).

One of the chemical substances that makes honey antibacterial is hydrogen peroxide, that old standby disinfectant sometimes still found in first-aid kits. It kills bacteria on contact but has fallen out of favor because it soon becomes ineffective when exposed to light and air, and because in high concentration it damages tissue. When diluted by the body fluids in a wound, honey continuously produces miniscule amounts of hydrogen peroxide. This slow-release mechanism forms enough hydrogen peroxide to kill bacteria but not enough to damage tissue.

The presence of antibacterial substances in honey is easily demonstrated by a classic technique of bacteriology—the same one by which Alexander Fleming discovered the bacteria-killing property of the mold penicillium, which is the source of penicillin, the first of the modern antibiotics. The method is simple. Bacteria are grown on a nutrient-containing agar gel in a covered Petri dish; a drop of the substance to be tested—honey in this case—is placed on the surface of the agar. If the honey, or some other substance, kills bacteria, a "halo" of bacteria-free surface surrounding the drop will appear.

Different kinds of honey, especially dark ones, contain antioxidants, which are important in nutrition because they prevent the formation of free radicals from fats. Free radicals can damage DNA, the stuff of the genes—damage that can ultimately lead to age-related diseases such as strokes, cancer, and arthritis. Honey also contains plant-derived substances known as flavonoids, which are probably important in the diet because they are believed to have a role in preventing inflammation and cancer.

Honey is prescribed by physicians as a medicine in Europe, New Zealand, Australia, and many other countries of the world—with the notable exception of the United States. Why is honey not used—and in fact is often derided—by the American medical community? My guess, and it's probably a good one, is that it's because honey is in the public domain. It cannot be patented. Consequently, pharmaceutical companies—with their eyes ever on the bottom line—have no interest in promoting honey as a medicine, presumably because they see little profit in it.

According to an Associated Press report of January 1, 2008, "Nature's Original Antibiotic Making Medical Comeback," however, the Canadian company Derma Sciences manufactures wound and burn dressings, Medihoney, based on manuka honey. These have been recently approved by the U.S. Food and Drug Administration, and their use by American physicians is steadily increasing—with many reports of success. An American physician who used Medihoney to treat badly burned children at a military clinic in Iraq reported that it is superior to the conventional dressing, according to the Associated Press story. The children healed more quickly and with fewer complications. He said, "I would use the Medihoney on burns on my children, as the first choice, without question."

There are other products of bees that have or may have medicinal value. The antibacterial value of propolis is impressively and convincingly illustrated by Majno's account of a mouse that entered a honey bee colony, was killed by the bees, and, because it was too large to remove from the hive, was covered with propolis. It was not decayed by bacteria, and eventually became mummified. Some think that bee stings alleviate the pain of arthritis, but this is dubious. Beeswax is a component of lip balms and cosmetics.

Burt's Bees Beeswax Lip Balm is thought by many to be the world's best lip balm. Royal jelly, secreted by workers and fed only to larvae destined to become queens, has been an ingredient in various cosmetics for women. The idea seems to be that royal jelly contains some mysterious substance that can make a larva become a "super" female—a fertile queen—rather than just another sterile female worker. If so, it has been mistakenly believed, it just might enhance the femininity of a woman. It turns out that royal jelly contains no mysterious "feminizing" substance. It just contains more sugar than the ordinary bee's milk workers secrete and feed to larvae destined to become mere sterile workers. The larva, stimulated by the extra sugar in royal jelly, eats more and grows larger. Growing up to be a queen is just a matter of eating more and getting bigger. Royal jelly will not enhance a woman's femininity.

My friends and colleagues David Nanney and Gene Robinson both tell me that the tiny fruit fly *Drosophila*—not white mice or rats—is the animal most frequently used in biological laboratory research. (This is the same little fly that appears when you have overripe fruit in your home.) There is no doubt that *Drosophila* was the most important laboratory animal in the development of classical genetics, setting the stage for the modern science of molecular genetics, which continues to use the tiny fruit fly as a research animal. At the beginning of the twentieth century, Thomas Hunt Morgan of Columbia University, one of the giants of classical genetics, made *Drosophila* the most important research animal in the field of genetics. He showed that the chromosomes in the nucleus of the cell bear the factors of heredity, the genes, which—although invisible—could be shown to exist. Today, molecular geneticists can locate specific genes on the long double-helical molecules of DNA, the major components of the chromosomes, and can determine their effects on anatomy, physiology, and behavior. Their work has had and is still having a huge impact on our understanding of life—how organisms evolve, function, and reproduce. Of particular interest to all of us is the contribution that the science of genetics has made to the advancement of medical knowledge and to our fundamental understanding of the immune system and genetic disorders such as cystic fibrosis, sickle-cell anemia, hemophilia, Tay-Sachs disease, and many others.

In chapter 1 we met insects that people like: the cute little ladybird beetles that charm us, the flashing fireflies that brighten the night, and the beautiful butterflies that grace our summer days. Now we turn to insects that entertain people or work behind the scenes in cultural institutions: singing katydids that are kept as pets in homes, fighting crickets on which people bet large sums of money, fleas that perform in circuses, and even, behind the scenes, hair- and flesh-eating beetles that museums and zoological laboratories use to clean skeletons.

X Insect Pets and Performers

Sometimes a field cricket would move into our home in autumn and take up residence in the fireplace in our family room. He was a welcome guest. We seldom saw him, but my wife, daughters, and I enjoyed his cheery chirping in the evening. (Don't fret! The cricket was gone before we used that fireplace.) Some people don't welcome crickets into their homes, probably because they equate them with cockroaches. But many do welcome them—especially in the Orient, as you will soon see, and more often than you might expect in Europe and North America. In Charles Dickens's *The Cricket on the Hearth,* a house cricket begins to chirp as Dot Peerybingle welcomes her husband home. The husband comments that "it's merrier than ever tonight," and Dot rejoices that "it's sure to bring us good fortune, John! To have a Cricket on the Hearth is the luckiest thing in all the world."

Our cricket was a big, shiny, black fellow with brown wings and long, graceful antennae. We knew he was a male because females don't chirp. Adult crickets and many other adult insects "sing" for the same reason that birds do—to warn away other males and to attract females. As is to be expected, both male and female crickets have ears, but they are located in what seems to us to be a most unusual place—one at the base of each of the longest segments of the front pair of legs. When a field cricket chirps, as we learn from John Henry Comstock, he raises his leathery, parchment-like front wings (wing covers) at an angle of about 45 degrees and produces his note by running a scraper on one wing along a file on the other wing. As Vincent Dethier put it in his delightful little book *Crickets and Katydids, Concerts and Solos,* "As the bow of a violin is drawn across the strings and sets them vibrating and as the body of the violin is set resonating by transmission of the vibrations through the bridge, so the cricket draws a scraper across a file of small teeth and sets the wing covers to resonating."

The cricket's name is onomatopoeic, derived from the sound it makes. Frank Cowan notes that "the English name *Cricket,* the French *Cri-Cri,* the Dutch *Krekel,* and the Welsh *Cricell,* . . . are evidently all derived from the *creak*-ing sounds of these insects."

Some crickets are known as "thermometer insects" because the frequency of their chirping indicates the air temperature. Because insects are cold-blooded, having no internal mechanism for controlling their body temperature—like frogs and lizards—the rate at which they sing or perform other activities varies with the air temperature. When it is warm, the rate at which they chirp is fast; when it is cold, the rate is slower. Therefore, the air temperature can be calculated from the frequency with which a cricket chirps. For example, Paul Villiard presented a formula for calculating the air temperature from the rate at which the common field cricket, the guest in my home, chirps. Count the number of chirps that a cricket makes in exactly fifteen seconds; that number plus fifty is the air temperature in degrees

Fahrenheit. Similarly, thirty-seven plus the number of chirps a snowy tree cricket makes in fifteen seconds is the Fahrenheit temperature.

The next time you amble through the countryside, especially near a hay field at the edge of a brushy area, stop to listen to the mixed chorus of crickets, grasshoppers, and katydids. Dethier wrote a delightful and insightful description of the insect music that was all around him in early summer in just such a place in New Hampshire:

> Since the balmy days of June, more musicians had gradually been added to the orchestra. The music had already developed a richness, complexity, and change of mood. New sounds, tempi, and sequences were being introduced. Admittedly, musical analogies are stretched because in the world of insects each instrument is a primitive device tuned to a single pitch. On the other hand, there are many kinds of instruments and thus many tones in the composition. There are also, when all things are considered, passages forte and pianissimo, choruses, solos, variations on themes. There are no melodies as such, no composer to orchestrate the whole, and no conductor to interpret and direct, but the ultimate expression is a paean of nature.

In 1898, Lafcadio Hearn, who then taught English literature at the Imperial University of Tokyo, wrote of the great love, much of which persists to this day, that the Japanese had for the natural world:

> But long before it became the fashion to keep singing-insects [in small cages], their music had been celebrated by poets as one of the aesthetic pleasures of the autumn. There are charming references to singing-insects in poetical collections made during the tenth century, and doubtless to many compositions of a yet earlier period. And just as places famous for cherry, plum, or other blossoming trees, are still regularly visited every year by thousands and tens of thousands, merely for the delight of seeing the flowers in

> their seasons,—so in ancient times city-dwellers made autumn excursions to country-districts simply for the pleasure of hearing the chirruping choruses of crickets and of locusts,—the night-singers especially.

It is widely known that the Japanese and the Chinese keep caged crickets and other insects in their homes for the pleasure of hearing them sing. I will say more about that later—after acquainting you with the little-known fact that in the nineteenth century this custom was not altogether unknown in Europe. In Spain, we read in Frank Cowan's book, "people of fashion" kept "a species of locust—called there *Gryllo*—in cages, *grillaria*—for the sake of its song," and, like canaries, they were kept in churches to sing during the celebration of mass. The "locust" was probably a cricket. Locusts, which are actually grasshoppers, don't have a particularly pleasing song. Furthermore, *Gryllo* and Gryllidae, the name of the cricket family, come from the same Latin root. We also learn from Hearn that the youth of Germany kept field crickets in small boxes made expressly for housing these singers. "They carry these boxes of crickets into their bed-rooms at night, and are soothed to sleep with their chirping lullaby."

The keeping of singing insects as pets probably originated in China and later spread to Japan. In 1928, Yin-Ch'i Hsu wrote: "Their beautiful and musical trills or 'songs' . . . [had] long attracted the attention of people in ancient China. Thereupon people began to keep crickets as interned prisoners in cages so as to enjoy their concert at any time." According to Berthold Laufer's 1927 pamphlet of the Field Museum of Natural History in Chicago, during the T'ang dynasty (618–906 C.E.) the Chinese began to keep caged crickets in order to enjoy their music. Early in the thirteenth century, during the Sung dynasty, Kia Se-tao, a minister of state, wrote the *Tsu Chi King* (*Book of Crickets*), which was still used in the nineteenth century. According to

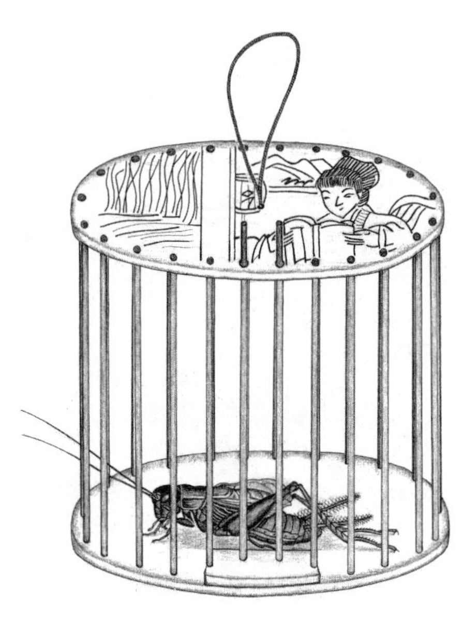

Laufer, "the author, a passionate cricket fancier himself, gave minute descriptions and subtle classifications of all species and varieties of crickets known to him and dwelt at length on their treatment and care." Laufer further reports:

> The praise of the cricket is sung in the odes of the *Shi king*, the earliest collection of Chinese popular songs. People then enjoyed listening to its chirping sounds, while it moved about in their houses or under their beds. It was regarded as a creature of good omen, and wealth was predicted for the families which had many crickets on their hearths. When their voices were heard in the autumn, it was a signal for the weavers to commence their work.
>
> The sounds produced by the mitred cricket . . . recall to the Chinese the

Above: Singing crickets, such as this one in a cage from China, are still cherished in both China and Japan.

click of a weaver's shuttle. One of its names therefore is *tsu-chi,* which means literally "one who stimulates spinning." "Chicken of the weaver's shuttle" is a term of endearment for it.

A Chinese book of the eighth century C.E. says that the "ladies of the palace" caught crickets in small golden cages and placed them near their pillows so they could hear them sing during the night. The common people used small cages made of bamboo or wood, some of which were veritable works of art. In later years, the cricket cages used during the winter months were made of gourds that were artificially—and often artistically—shaped by forcing them to develop in a clay mold. The flower from which the gourd would develop was thrust into the mold, and as the gourd grew it had to assume the sometimes fanciful shape of the mold. Gourd cages made for the palace bore designs in high relief formed by patterns deeply incised into the inner surface of their molds. Men sometimes carried gourd and cricket tucked into their clothing wherever they went. Laufer noted that "in passing men in the street you may hear the shrill sound of the insect from its warm and safe place of refuge." In summer some of the well-to-do hung from their belts crickets housed in elaborately carved walnut shells.

Crickets were for sale in the markets of China in the 1920s and long before that. (Recently, Ying Wang, a Chinese graduate student in the University of Illinois Department of Entomology, assured me that singing insects in decorative cages, especially katydids, are still for sale in China.) In former times, people raised crickets in their homes by the hundreds and sometimes had several rooms stacked with the clay jars that housed them in summer. Prosperous "cricket ranchers" hired experts to look after their stock. In summer, the crickets were usually fed fresh cucumber, lettuce, and other greens. In winter, when they were kept in gourds, they were generally fed masticated chestnuts and yellow beans, although in the south of China they were also given chopped fish, various kinds of insects, and even a little honey as a "tonic."

As we are guided by Hearn on a stroll among the vendors' booths at a temple festival in Tokyo on a night in the late nineteenth century, we see vendors selling many beautiful and, to us, exotic things. We see booths displaying splendorous, colorful toys; images of demons, gods, and goblins; immense lantern transparencies painted with monstrous faces; and also "a booth illuminated like a magic-lantern, and stocked with tiny wooden cages out of which an incomparable shrilling proceeds." This is the booth of a vendor of singing insects, and the shrilling noise is a mixed chorus of crickets and other musical insects. In the aesthetic life of the Japanese, "a most refined and artistic people, these insects hold a place not less important or well-deserved than that occupied in Western Civilization by our thrushes, linnets, nightingales and canaries."

In Japan, the recorded history of keeping singing insects as pets goes back almost a thousand years. Hearn quotes a passage from a work titled *Chomon-Shū:*

> On the twelfth day of the eighth month of the second year of Kaho [1095 C.E.], the Emperor ordered his pages and chamberlains to go to Sagano and find some insects. The Emperor gave them a cage of network of bright purple thread.... On reaching Sagano ... the party sent their attendants to catch the insects. In the evening they returned to the palace.... The cage was respectfully presented to the Empress. There was *sake*-drinking in the palace that evening; and many poems were composed. The Empress and her court ladies joined in the making of the poems.

According to Hearn, in Tokyo, the "regular trade" in musical insects began late in the eighteenth century, and by 1897 twelve kinds of crickets and other singing insects could be purchased there. By then there were several prominent dealers and breeders, and a multitude of itinerant vendors who did business mainly at temple festivals, which were celebrated in some quarter of the city almost every night of the year.

"But even today," reports Hearn, "city-dwellers, when giving a party, will sometimes place cages of singing insects among the garden shrubbery, so that the guests may enjoy not only the music of the little creatures, but also those memories or sensations of rural peace which such music evokes."

Among the most beloved of the singing insects is the *suzumushi* (*suzu,* bell; *mushi,* insect), or bell insect, which is still popular in China. Its sound, says Hearn, is like that of a very small bell, "or a bunch of little bells such as a Shinto priestess uses in the sacred dances." He translates a lovely Japanese poem about this renowned musical insect:

> Hark to those tinkling tones,—the chant of the suzumushi!
> —if a jewel of dew could sing, it would tinkle with such a voice!

The Kōrogi, a night cricket, is mentioned in the *Manyōshu,* the oldest known collection of Japanese poetry, which was probably compiled in the eighth century C.E.:

> Niwa-kusa ni
> Murasamé furite
> Kōrogi no
> Naku oto Kikeba
> Aki tsukinikery

Hearn translates:

> Showers have sprinkled the garden-grass. Hearing the sound of the crying of the Kōrogi, I know that the autumn has come.

A large, green katydid commonly sold in Tokyo in Hearn's day, the *kutsuwamushi* (bridle-bit insect), is named for its song, "which resembles the jingling and ringing of the old-fashioned Japanese bridle-bit. . . . Heard from far away at night the sound is pleasant, and is really so much like the ringing of a bridle-bit of a horse, that when you first listen to it you cannot but feel how much real poetry belongs to the name of this insect." What is probably the oldest poem on the *kutsuwamushi* was written by Idzumi-Shikibu (and translated by Hearn):

> Waga Seko wa
> Koma ni makasété
> Kinikeri to
> Kiku ni kikasuru
> Kutsuwamushi kana!
>
> Listen!—his bridle rings;—that is surely my husband
> Homeward hurrying now—fast as the horse can bear him!
> Ah! My ear was deceived! Only the Kutsuwamushi!

According to Robert Pemberton, the Japanese still enjoy the songs of caged insects, but the elaborate ancient "cricket culture" of the Japanese described by Hearn in 1898 has diminished and been modernized. The finely crafted and beautiful cages made of twigs, slivers of bamboo, or wire have been replaced by clear plastic terrariums. A few species of singing insects and plastic terrariums along with packaged soil and insect food are sold in pet shops. An electronic katydid that mimics the song of the real insect is available for a few dollars. A superior electronic device with a more true-to-life rendition of the song of the famous bell insect, the black tree cricket, was sold for the equivalent of two hundred U.S. dollars in 1990 in a Tokyo Mitsukoshi department store. Recordings of various singing insects are sold in record stores and can be heard in subway stations and other public places.

In China, but not in Japan, cricket fights have been a widely popular entertainment since the Sung dynasty (960–1278 C.E.). For many, cricket fights are not merely an entertainment; they are a passion and probably often an addiction for those who bet money—sometimes large sums—on the outcome of a fight. In Canton (now Guangzhou), according to Hsu, at a single match an aggregate of as much as one hundred thousand dollars may be wagered by the owners of the crickets and the spectators. He does not tell us whether or not these are U.S. dollars.

Before we proceed with a consideration of fighting crickets, we should digress to ask why crickets sing and fight. That is, of what biological value—if any—are singing and fighting in the life of a cricket in nature? The short answer is that it's all about sex and reproduction. Male field crickets, we learn from Robert and Janice Matthews, have a repertoire of two quite different songs. The familiar chirping is a loud "calling song" that attracts females to the male's burrow. After mating, the female leaves to insert her eggs into the soil with a long, spear-shaped ovipositor. The other song, the "aggressive rivalry song," which is less loud, not often heard, and distinctly different from the calling song, is sung by both males when a rival arrives to challenge the resident for possession of the burrow. The loser of the ensuing fight flees.

With a clever series of experiments, L. H. Phillips II and M. Konishi found that the aggressive rivalry song has a powerful intimidating effect on male crickets. They first painted identifying marks on a large number of males and then placed pairs of previously unacquainted males in cages so small that they frequently encountered each other and fought. After observing many fights, they deafened the habitual losers by incapacitating the ears on their front legs after anesthetizing them. Then they rematched the deafened losers with the crickets that had defeated them and had not been deafened. In these contests, the former subordinate males, the losers, defeated their former vanquishers almost every time! The most likely explanation for this is that the deaf crickets were not intimidated by their opponents' songs because they could not hear them. On the other hand, the males that had not been deafened lost the fights because they were intimidated by the songs of their rivals, which, although deaf, were not mute. To the best of my knowledge, the handlers of fighting crickets have not—at least not yet—deafened their crickets to make champions of them.

Good fighting crickets are greatly valued: "Choice champions," according to Laufer, "fetch prices up to $100, the value of a good horse in China." They are given meticulous care. Their usual diet is a bit of rice mixed with fresh cucumbers, boiled chestnuts, lotus seeds, and mosquitoes. Some cricket fanciers let mosquitoes bite them, and when the mosquitoes are engorged with blood they feed them to their most promising fighters. Expert cricket handlers, according to Laufer, know a great deal about the diseases of crickets and have remedies, which may or may not work, for their treatment. Crickets sick from overeating are fed on "a kind of red insect." If sickness is thought to be caused by cold, they are given mosquitoes; if by heat, they are given shoots of the green pea.

"The tournaments take place in an open space, a public square, or in a special house termed Autumn Amusements," Laufer reports. A pottery jar, the arena, is placed on a table covered with silk cloth. The two contestants are evenly matched, and carefully weighed on tiny scales before they are pitted against each other. If they are reluctant to fight, the referee, the "director of the battle," spurs them on by stroking and poking them with a "tickler" made of a rat or hare whisker inserted in a reed, bone, or ivory handle, which is kept in a bamboo or wooden tube, although "the rich indulge in the luxury of having an elegant ivory tube surmounted by the carving of a lion." Eventually, the two combatants fight each other mercilessly. Most fights end with the death of one of them, often because "the more agile or stronger pounces . . . on the body of its opponent, severing its head completely."

A champion, Hsu tells us, is given tender loving care after a match:

> Three to five days should be allowed for the fighters to rest after combat. In case the insects have fought thirty or forty rounds, seven days should be allowed. Those which are badly injured, should be separated from the females for one or two days. Closer attention should be given to those winners who fought only one round, and they should not be allowed to fight again without the following treatment: After the fight they should be allowed to take a bath in the juice of the duck-weed (*Lemna*) . . . and then in clean water. Equal volumes of child's urine and clear water should be provided in the water dish. The females should be separated out for two or three days. The winners will then recover their original fighting capacity. Those with their jaws injured should be fed with child's urine and water also.

And, as Hsu goes on to say, when a champion dies, it is put to rest with a befitting funeral. "A cricket, which wins many victories, is honored with the title of 'ever victorious general.' After its death, it is placed in a small silver coffin, and is solemnly buried. It is believed that the owner of the champion will have good luck and will find excellent fighters during the next year in the vicinity where his favorite cricket is buried."

As Laufer eloquently describes, victories are enthusiastically celebrated:

> The names of the victorious champions are inscribed on an ivory tablet . . . and these tablets like diplomas are religiously kept in the houses of the fortunate owners. Sometimes the characters of the inscription are laid out in gold. The victory is occasion for great rejoicing and jollification. Music is performed, gongs are clanged, flags displayed, flowers scattered, and the tablet of victory is triumphantly marched in front, [and] the jubilant victor struts in the procession of his overjoyed compatriots, carrying his victorious cricket home. The sunshine of his glory falls on the whole community in which he lives, and his village will gain as much publicity and notoriety as an American town which has produced a golf or baseball champion.

Ying Wang tells me that cricket fighting is still popular in China today. While Zao Zedong (Mao Tse-tung) was the chairman of the Communist Party of the People's Republic of China, from 1949 to 1976, cricket fighting was discouraged, although, as D. K. M. Kevan and C. C. Hsiung tell us, at that time there were still many people in the British dependency of Hong Kong who indulged in the sport of cricket fighting for the purpose of gambling. Wang says that gambling is illegal in China today, but I am willing to bet that clandestine gambling flourishes, just as it does everywhere else in the world.

Pet insects are not nearly as popular in the United States as are pet crickets in China and Japan, but there are a few insects that some Americans—and Canadians, too—find pleasure in keeping as pets. Ant "farms" are popular, especially with children. They can look through the glass sides of the farm and watch with fascination the many activities of the busy ants as they scurry through their tunnels. Some people build homemade ant farms that they stock with ants they capture themselves; there are clear directions in Michael Tweedie's *Pleasure from Insects.* But it is, of course, much easier to buy an ant farm and the ants with which to stock it. Pet shops often have them. For example, a pet shop in Champaign, Illinois, sells them for about $30. Many dealers can be found on the Internet, including some that offer do-it-yourself kits.

Raising silkworms can be an entertaining and educational experience for both older children and adults. Eggs are available from biological supply houses. Although the caterpillars require frequent attention, they are actually fairly easy to raise because, as we saw in chapter 2, they have been so completely domesticated that they don't have to be caged. They will not wander away from their food until they are full-grown and ready to spin a cocoon. I have already described a rather complicated method for raising silkworms on a commercial scale, but Paul Villiard explains a much simpler method for raising a small number of them as a hobby. They can be kept in any shallow pan, which need not be covered, and fed fresh leaves cut from a white mulberry tree. (They will starve to death rather than eat anything else.) As the leaves in the tray are consumed, just lay fresh leaves right on top of the caterpillars. But be warned! When small, the larvae eat very little, but when they grow large, they are voracious and will need to be fed a lot of leaves—many more than you might expect. During the last eight days of its larval life, a silkworm caterpillar will eat about 95 percent of its total intake of leaves! Every few days, the caterpillar droppings should be dumped from the pan. When the caterpillars begin to wander, they are ready to spin their cocoons, which they will do in an egg carton or a bundle of twigs that is placed near them ahead of time.

The giant hissing cockroach from Madagascar (*Gromphadorhina portenosa*) can almost always be seen in insect zoos and is always a big hit. According to Robert Barth, this exceptionally large insect—males may be as much as 4 inches long—is heavy-bodied and wingless and lives under debris on the forest floor. Like all but a tiny minority of the approximately thirty-five hundred known species of cockroaches, this handsome insect is never a household pest. One of its claims to fame is the loud hissing noise, made by expelling air from two of the openings to the respiratory system, that males make when alarmed or doing battle with each other. This species also has an unusual method of reproduction. As with all other cockroaches, Louis Roth tells us, its eggs are contained in a capsule that is extruded from the female's body, but unlike with most other species, the capsule is withdrawn back into the "uterus," or brood sac, until the embryos are fully developed and ready to hatch.

Most of the beetles of the family Dermestidae, variously known as carpet, hide, skin, or larder beetles, feed—varying with the species—on carrion, leather, furs, woolens, stored foods, or other organic substances, including even dried insect specimens. "This is one group of insects," write Donald Borror and his coauthors, "that every entomology student will sooner or later encounter. All he has to do to get some dermestids is to make an insect collection and not protect it against these pests." In museums, dermestids of the genus *Anthrenus,* small insects only about a tenth of an inch long—often known as museum beetles—feed on and thereby damage not only dry insect specimens but also the unprotected dry skins of birds and mammals. You might consider this as the revenge of the insects. As we will soon see, however, museum curators have put a close relative of the "avengers," a species of the genus *Dermestes,* to work removing the flesh from skeletons of birds and mammals. At a length of about a third of an inch, the skeleton-cleaning beetles are considerably larger than the museum beetles.

In nature, both of these beetles feed on carrion. The little museum beetles, which prefer to feed on fur, feathers, and bits of dry, mummified flesh, do not arrive on a carcass until all of the moist flesh has been removed by maggots and other insects.

Most museums maintain large colonies of the skeleton-cleaning dermestids, much as described by E. Raymond Hall and W. C. Russell in 1933. At that time, sheep's heads or other flesh was used to maintain the colony when the beetles did not have a specimen on which to feed. Today, the beetles are fed dry dog food. A specimen to be skeletonized, a squirrel for example, is skinned and eviscerated, and then much of the flesh is removed before it is placed in a container that houses many thousands of dermestids. Both the adult and larval beetles feed on the body of the squirrel, but most of the work is done by the larvae, which are, of course, growing rapidly and therefore require much more food than the adults. A small specimen, such as a mouse or the skull of a rat, may be thoroughly defleshed in a day or two. A larger specimen, such as the body of a seal, may require a week or two.

In his fascinating book on forensic entomology, *A Fly for the Prosecution,* M. Lee Goff points out that *Dermestes,* the "skeleton cleaners," arrive on a carcass only after it starts to dry out. This has led to the false assumption that they will not feed on fresh flesh. Nevertheless, these skeleton cleaners are perfectly willing to feed on moist flesh, but in nature are usually prevented from doing so by competition from hordes of other insects, particularly maggots.

Goff explains that the decomposition of a dead animal, the return of its molecules to the soil, is effected by a succession of different kinds of insects and microbes, which begins when blow flies, especially blue bottles, begin to lay eggs on the body, often within minutes of death. Thousands of blow fly maggots consume most of the flesh. They are succeeded in stages by other insects. The last are hide beetles, or carpet beetles, which eat the last scraps of dry skin and hair clinging to the bare bones, which are ultimately consumed by rodents and certain insects.

Understanding this succession makes it possible to determine the time of death of a human whose corpse has been exposed for days, weeks, or even months, too long to be dated by a medical examiner. An actual case is recounted by Wayne Lord. A fully clothed, almost skeletonized body of a man was found by the side of a road. An autopsy showed that he had died of natural causes. The body was to be identified by searching the missing persons files for the period during which he had died. Judging only by the appearance of the remains, medical examiners concluded that death had occurred two to three months before the corpse had been found. Searching the records for that period would have been futile. A forensic entomologist found living blow fly pupae with the corpse, indicating that it could have been exposed for no more than thirty-five days, and a more detailed entomological analysis indicated that death had occurred thirty days before the discovery of the body. When the remains were identified, it was found that the decedent was last seen hitchhiking near the death scene thirty-one days before the body was discovered.

P. T. Barnum believed that a circus just has to have elephants, big elephants like his famous Jumbo. Even so, there used to be circuses that drew small but appreciative audiences even though the performers were just tiny fleas. What was for many years the last flea circus in the United States—perhaps anywhere in the world—closed in the late 1950s when its impresario died. I saw that miniature circus in an amusement arcade on Forty-second Street near Broadway in New York. The performance was staged on a round table around which a dozen or so people could stand. I don't remember much about the performance, but I do recall being very impressed by the astounding strength of the tiny, barely visible fleas. One flea by itself was capable of pulling some heavy object, such as a miniature model of a wagon, which was at least hundreds of times its size.

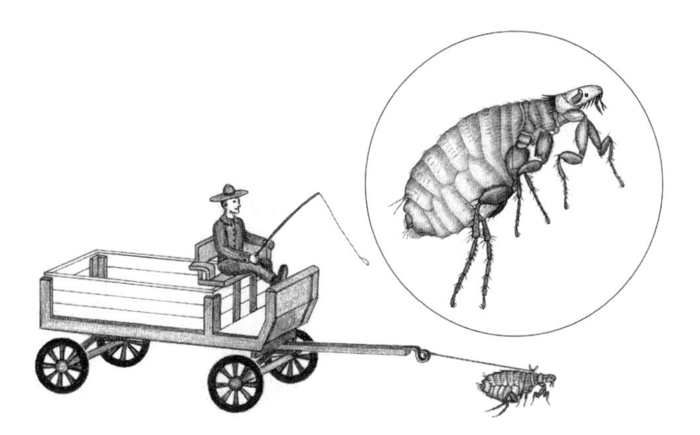

The history of performing fleas goes back many years. Cowan quotes a Mr. Bingley who wrote that in London in 1745 "an ingenious watchmaker in the Strand, exhibited . . . a little ivory chaise with four wheels, and all its proper apparatus, and the figure of a man sitting on the box, all of which were drawn by a single Flea." In England in 1830, at a fair in Kent, a man exhibited three fleas harnessed to a carriage that they pulled with great ease, a pair that drew a chariot, and a single flea that pulled a brass cannon. "The exhibitor showed the whole first act through a magnifying glass, and then to the naked eye; so that all were satisfied there was no deception," Cowan recounts.

In 1877, W. H. Dall noticed a sign that proclaimed "Exhibition of Educated Fleas" over a doorway on Broadway near East Sixteenth Street in New York. Dall recalled that during his boyhood the tales of the marvelous performances of supposedly educated fleas had for him "a peculiar interest not unmixed with incredulity." He went in to see the exhibition. After watching the performance, he concluded that the fleas were not trained or educated in

Above: A flea performing in a flea circus pulls a tiny model wagon many times its own weight.

any way, and that all of their performances were the result of the restrained insects' efforts to escape.

Each flea wore a "harness" that tied it to some object in such a way as not to hinder the movements of its legs. The harness was a silk fiber that encircled the flea's "neck" and was knotted on its upper side. A bristle or a fine wire that could attach the flea to an object of some sort was cemented to the knot. Only females were used, Dall explained, because the males are much smaller and "excessively mulish and altogether disinclined to work." The performing fleas were nourished by sucking blood from the "ring master's" skin and lived, on average, for about eight months.

Single fleas pulled tiny and beautifully made models of various sorts, among them a horsecar, a coach, a wheelbarrow, and even a butterfly. Small bits of tissue paper, silk, or some other light material attached to the knot on the insect's back served as a dress or other item of clothing. Dall found the dancing fleas the most amusing and, at first, the most incomprehensible of all the flea circus performances. An orchestra consisted of a group of fleas attached head-side-up by their harness wire to the top side of a small music box. The vibrations that the box made while playing caused the fleas to "gesticulate violently, giving the illusion that they were playing musical instruments. Below them several pairs of fleas (fastened by a little bar to each other in pairs, those of each couple just so far apart that they cannot touch each other) are apparently waltzing; . . . the two composing each pair are pointed in opposite ways; each tries to run away, the 'parallelogram of forces' is produced; the forward intention, converted to a rotary motion ludicrously imitating [a waltz]."

The flea circus made a comeback a decade ago—apparently as a work of installation art. The January 16, 1999, issue of Toronto's *National Post* reported that Maria Fernanda Cardoso, an installation artist who had previously "created a sprawling web of dried starfish that hung throughout the gallery space in hexagonal clusters," recreated the flea circus and billed it as the world's only flea circus. Among her performers were Bounce 1 and Bounce 2, flea cannonballs that were shot out of tiny cannons. As Brutus, billed as the world's strongest flea, pulled a tiny locomotive about one thousand times his size, "Cardoso proffers an accompanying monologue full of deadpan humour and double entendres." She was invited to exhibit her circus at the exhibition for the opening of the New Museum in New York and at Scottsdale's Contemporary Arts Museum's Celebration of the Millennium in Arizona.

EPILOGUE

The Ecological Context

We have considered insects mainly as creatures that please us or are directly useful to us in some way. Fireflies flashing in the night are a delight to watch, the cheerful song of the cricket on the hearth charms the ear, and the honey that bees make from the sweet nectar of flowers pleases the palate. Insects are much more than that, though, and I want to broaden our view of the natural world by briefly viewing insects from another perspective: as animals that live in the real world of complex ecosystems, in which they depend on and interact with a multitude of different kinds of plants and animals. In order to survive in its ecosystem from generation to generation, an insect or any other animal species must eat and grow, avoid being eaten, and bear the next generation of offspring. Following are a few examples of the ways in which some insects—mainly species you met in the preceding chapters—strive to fulfill these three fundamental requirements for survival.

Among the insects we have considered are plant feeders, such as the silk moth; predators that eat other insects, such as the giant water bug and the paper wasps; a scavenger, the dung-feeding scarab; and the blood-sucking flea. The giant water bug, that gastronomic delicacy of Southeast Asia, itself savors aquatic insects of all sorts and even small fish and tadpoles. It and its relatives—some of which occur in North America—are fiercely efficient predators. Like praying mantises, they use their raptorial front legs to snatch and grab their prey. Although the mouthparts of most insects are of the chewing type, those of the giant water bugs—like those of fleas, aphids, mosquitoes, and quite a few other insects—are modified for piercing and sucking. Giant water bugs are also among the insects that practice extraoral digestion, a fascinating physiological process of which most people have never heard. They inject their prey with a venom that kills it and with digestive fluids that liquefy its muscles and other internal organs. Then they suck up this predigested meal. Adult paper wasps, which have mouthparts capable of both chewing and licking, feed on nectar and honeydew themselves but feed insects to their larvae. They seldom sting their prey, but rather kill it by biting its neck. (But they do sting fiercely in defense of the nest.) The wasps skin and disembowel caterpillars and carry the remaining wad of muscle tissue to the nest and feed it to the larvae. The offal left behind, usually on the upper surface of a leaf, serves as a snack for flies.

About 45 percent of the insects feed on plants—very few on mosses or ferns, some on conifers such as pines and firs, and the majority on flowering plants ranging from oaks and maples to cabbages and sunflowers. Of the approximately 400,000 plant-feeding insects, about 320,000 are specialists that, like the mulberry silkworm, feed on a few plants of only one family or of a few closely related families. Such strict specialist species greatly outnumber generalists that will feed on many different kinds of unrelated plants. Why is it that so many insects, surrounded by hundreds of potential food plants, pass up so many that are successfully used by other insects? It does pay to specialize, to evolve so as to best cope with just one or a few plants by adapting to their particular attributes. But the much more important part of the answer is probably the escalating "arms race" between plants and the insects that feed on them.

Some plants defend themselves with thorns or spines, but their major weapons are biochemical. A mutation may provide a plant with a new, noxious biochemical that has no role in its physiology but deters insects that attempt to feed on it. Insects have, of course, evolved ways to get around plants' chemical defenses. If their host plant adds a new chemical to its arsenal, they must find a way to live with it, switch to another species of plant, or go extinct. But with a bit of luck, a genetic mutation will enable them to detoxify the new feeding deterrent or to avoid its effects in some other way, and they may even come to use its taste or odor to recognize the host plant. A plant is likely to fight back with yet another defensive chemical, and the insect may well respond by evolving a way to deal with this new defense. Over eons, a succession of such reciprocal responses, an arms race, has resulted in the accumulation of tens of thousands of these biochemicals in the plant kingdom. Some of these substances are perceptible to us and give plants their characteristic odor or taste. Just as we recognize cabbage, celery, mint, and thyme by their odor and taste, specialist insects recognize their host plants by means of such substances, many of which are imperceptible to us.

Adult bees, butterflies, and many other insects collect nectar, pollen, or both to feed themselves or to nourish their offspring. Flowering plants and their insect pollinators have evolved to accommodate each other. Plants attract insects with scents and colorful blossoms; most pollinators have color vision and an acute sense of smell. Plants produce nectar and extra pollen to reward pollinators; bees have spiny "baskets" on their hind legs to hold pollen, and most pollinators have sucking or lapping mouthparts for gathering nectar. About 160,000 species (78 percent) of the green plants, the only organisms that can harness the sun's energy to produce food, more or less depend on insects for pollination, and without them would go extinct or survive only as greatly reduced populations—an ecological catastrophe, because these plants are the foundation of most terrestrial ecosystems.

Insects are food not only for spiders, fish, toads, lizards, birds, and mammals, but also for an array of predaceous insects. How, then, do insects avoid being eaten? Lac insects, for example, hide in their shelters, and locusts and crickets leap away with their powerful hind legs. But I will tell you about one of the most fascinating ways in which insects avoid becoming a predator's meal.

Although most insects escape the notice of birds and other insect eaters because they are camouflaged and blend in with the background, some make themselves conspicuous with their bright colors. Monarch butterflies are orange and black; bald-faced hornets are black with white markings; honey bees have alternating orange and black bands; bumblebees are bold black and bright yellow. These insects make themselves conspicuous because they have effective defenses against predators, which soon learn to recognize and avoid them. Monarchs, for example, contain a toxin, which they sequester from their food plants, that makes birds vomit. The wasps, the honey bee, and the bumblebees have painful venomous stings.

As you know, the harmless drone fly's uncanny resemblance to the venomous honey bee tricks birds into passing it up as a meal. Bluffing of this sort, known as Batesian mimicry in honor of Henry Bates, the nineteenth-century naturalist who discovered this phenomenon, is widespread among the insects. Many perfectly edible butterflies mimic noxious butterflies; certain flies, moths, and even beetles mimic stinging bees or wasps; in the Philippines some defenseless cockroaches (which are not household pests) closely resemble inedible red and black ladybird beetles; in South America an acid-spraying bombardier beetle is mimicked by an edible cricket.

Yellow jackets, social paper-making wasps related to the bald-faced hornet, are mimicked—with frightening accuracy—by a large hover fly, *Spilomyia hamifera,* which has no common name. Not only does *Spilomyia* mimic the flagrantly conspicuous yellow-and-black color pattern of these wasps but it also mimics several of their anatomical and behavioral characteristics. While most flies are broad-waisted, *Spilomyia*'s waist is somewhat narrowed, as are the waists of these wasps. Like most other flies, it has short, stubby antennae barely visible to the naked eye, but it mimics the long, black, mobile antennae of the wasps by waving its black anterior legs in front of its head. As the wasps lap nectar from flowers, their tinted wings, folded lengthwise in several layers, are held out to the side and look like dark brown bands. *Spilomyia* cannot fold its wings, but it holds them out to the side, mimicking the appearance of the wasp's folded wing with a band of dark brown pigment along the leading edge of its otherwise transparent wing. Perched on a flower, the wasp makes itself even more conspicuous by rocking from side to side. *Spilomyia* mimics this movement by wagging its wings. Finally, if the fly is grasped by the fingers, or presumably by a bird's beak, it makes a loud sound acoustically virtually identical to the squawk of a disturbed wasp.

Finding a mate may be difficult for an insect because a member of the opposite sex may be far away. Many insects overcome this difficulty by emitting a sex attractant signal that can be perceived from a distance. Only three of the five senses are capable of perceiving distant signals: vision, hearing, and smell. All three are used by insects to bring the sexes together: for instance, visual signals by fireflies; sound by crickets and katydids; and pheromones, scents, by the mulberry silk moth, the giant silk moths, and the tiny lac insect.

Although our North American fireflies are loners, in Southeast Asia, as we have seen, there are gregarious fireflies that gather in trees by the tens of thousands and flash in synchrony. A firefly tree on the bank of a river can be seen from a boat that is miles away, but even in a dense forest the glow of a firefly tree flashing on and off is visible from far away. These trees are beacons that attract both males and females from a distance. Although both sexes produce light, only males flash brightly and in nearly perfect synchrony. But during the half-second interval between the males' flashes, the females' much dimmer light can be seen. They are probably informing the males of the presence of willing sex partners. After they have been inseminated, the females leave the tree to distribute their eggs in places where the predaceous larvae will find food.

Crickets, as you know, produce sound by stridulating, rubbing a scraper on one front wing against a file on the other front wing. Katydids sing in a similar fashion, but locusts and other grasshoppers stridulate by rubbing a long row of pegs on the hind leg against a forewing. Male crickets generally sing from the mouths of their burrows. Some amplify their chirps by digging the mouth of the burrow in the shape of a megaphone or a band shell. Opportunistic male crickets may approach a singing male with the intention of expropriating a female attracted to his song. These so-called satellite males lurk near a singing male but remain silent although they are perfectly capable of singing.

A sex attractant pheromone released by a female moth drifts downwind with the breeze, and as it spreads out, it assumes the shape of an irregular plume. A male that flies into this pheromone trail changes his course to fly upwind, but if he happens to blunder out of the plume, he flies about at random and may manage to reenter the plume. If he does, he continues to fly upwind until he comes to the female. To find her he need do no more than fly upwind. He is not guided by the increasing concentration of the pheromone as he approaches her.

Jim Sternburg and I used traps baited with a pheromone-releasing female cecropia moth to recapture marked males that we had released at various distances from the traps. The point was to find out from how far away a male, by a combination of random and pheromone-directed flight, can find a female. This bears on the question of how small and dispersed a population can be without going extinct. On a June morning in 1969, I saw the amazing spectacle of 204 beautiful male cecropias with 4- to 5-inch wingspans clinging to the screen walls of a large trap in my backyard. During the last few hours before dawn, a sex attractant emitted by the bait female had wafted downwind and was perceived by scent receptors on the males' large, feathery antennae. In the trap were several marked males that had come from more than 4 miles away and one from almost 8 miles away. But the distance record is held by a male promethea moth, another of the giant silkworms, that was caught in a trap baited with a female promethea almost 23 miles away, as the crow flies, from where he had been released three days earlier.

Parental care, broadly defined, is not at all uncommon among the insects. Among those we have met, the most painstaking caregivers are the social species: termites, ants, honey bees, and colonial wasps, whose offspring are dependent on the workers of the colony from egg to the molt to the adult stage. As we saw in chapter 6, E. O. Wilson, the famed conservationist and authority on ants, writes: "In Japanese the word 'ant' is intricately written by linking two characters: one meaning 'insect,' the other meaning 'loyalty,'" in recognition of how closely bound and "loyal" these social insects are to one another. Of the nonsocial insects, plant feeders such as butterflies and our native wild silk moths offer the bare minimum of care by laying their eggs on the appropriate plants, plants that the larvae, when hatched, will be willing to eat. The Egyptian scarab does much more: the larva feeds on a large ball of dung that its mother buries in the soil. The giant hissing cockroach of Madagascar retains her egg capsule in her body until the embryos are fully developed and ready to hatch. We have not considered the infamous tsetse fly, which transmits sleeping sickness in Africa, but I cannot resist telling you about its amazing reproductive behavior. The female retains a single egg in an analogue of the uterus. When the larva hatches, it suckles on milk—chemically much like the milk of a human or some other mammal—that is secreted into the uterus. When the larva is full-grown, the mother gives birth to it and it burrows into the soil to pupate.

The giant water bug of Southeast Asia and its relatives, some of which probably live in a pond near your home, give parental care in a most unusual way. In a closely related North American species, the female glues a hundred or more eggs to her mate's back. The male, who usually stays at the bottom of the pond if he bears no eggs, spends a great deal of time perched on a plant near the surface so as to expose the tips of the eggs to the air, and frequently wipes the eggs with his hind legs, presumably to remove mold spores. In an experiment, more than 90 percent of the eggs that remained on a father's back hatched, but all of the eggs that were removed and placed in a dish of water became infested with fungus and died within a week.

At one time it was supposed that the male is an unwilling victim of the female and, "embarrassed" by this enforced servitude, tries to wipe the eggs off his back with his hind legs. Years later, when natural selection and evolution had become the undisputed central theme of biology, it was pointed out that the "humiliated male hypothesis" is absurd because natural selection would not have favored females that dispose of their eggs on the back of a male only to have them discarded in places where they might not survive.

As I promised in the introduction, this book is about insects that we like or that are materially useful to us. They are considered in the first ten chapters. In the main, very little has been said about the ecological context of their lives and how they manage to survive in ecosystems that offer both opportunities and hazards, leaving these fascinating creatures in a biological limbo. To me, a retired professor of entomology, that is not a good thing. I hope that this epilogue, though necessarily brief, has given you a glimpse of the ecological context in which fireflies, honey bees, silk moths, and the others live and evolve. This brief glimpse only hints at the mind-blowing and not yet fully understood complexity of the many communities of plants and animals that inhabit our planet and of the indispensable roles that insects play in these communities, these ecosystems that together constitute the environment in which we live—the environment that is your and my only home.

Selected References

INTRODUCTION

Cowan, F. 1865. *Curious Facts in the History of Insects.* Philadelphia: J. B. Lippincott.

Lutz, F. E. 1918. *Field Book of Insects.* New York: G. P. Putnam's Sons. (Reprinted 1935.)

1. INSECTS PEOPLE LIKE

Boettner, G. H., J. S. Elkinton, and C. J. Boettner. 2000. Effects of a biological control introduction on three nontarget native species of saturniid moths. *Conservation Biology* 14:1798–1806.

Booth, M., and M. M. Allen. 1990. Butterfly garden design. In *Butterfly Gardening,* ed. Xerces Society and Smithsonian Institution, pp. 63–93. San Francisco: Sierra Club Books.

Buck, J. B. 1938. Synchronous rhythmic flashing of fireflies. *Quarterly Review of Biology* 13:301–314.

Campbell, A., and D. S. Noble, eds. 1993. *Japan: An Illustrated Encyclopedia,* vol. 1. Tokyo: Kodansha.

Cherry, R. H. 1993. Insects in the mythology of Native Americans. *American Entomologist* 39:16–21.

Comstock, J. H. 1950. *An Introduction to Entomology,* 9th edition, revised. Ithaca, NY: Comstock Publishing Company.

Dinesen, I. 1937. *Out of Africa.* New York: Modern Library.

Dunkle, S. 2000. *Dragonflies through Binoculars.* Oxford: Oxford University Press.

Hamilton, E. 1953. *Mythology.* New York: New American Library of World Literature.

Hearn, L. 1910. *A Japanese Miscellany.* Boston: Little, Brown, and Company.

Hogue, C. L. 1987. Cultural entomology. *Annual Review of Entomology* 32:181–199.

Kevan, P. G., and R. A. Bye. 1991. The natural history, sociobiology, and ethnobiology of *Eucheira socialis* Westwood (Lepidoptera: Pieridae), a unique and little-known butterfly from Mexico. *The Entomologist* 110:146–165.

Koller, L. 1963. *The Treasury of Angling.* New York: Golden Press.

Liu, G. 1939. Some extracts from the history of entomology in China. *Psyche* 46:23–28.

Lloyd, J. E. 1975. Aggressive mimicry in *Photuris* fireflies: Signal repertoires by femmes fatales. *Science* 187:452–453.

Lutz, F. E. 1918. *Field Book of Insects.* New York: G. P. Putnam's Sons. (Reprinted 1935.)

Milne, L., and M. Milne. 1980. *National Audubon Society Field Guide to North American Insects and Spiders.* New York: Alfred A. Knopf.

Peigler, R. S. 1993. Wild silks of the world. *American Entomologist* 39:151–161.

Rothschild, M. 1990. Gardening with butterflies. In *Butterfly Gardening,* ed. Xerces Society and Smithsonian Institution, pp. 7–15. San Francisco: Sierra Club Books.

Russell, S. A. 2003. *An Obsession with Butterflies.* New York: Basic Books.

Simon, H. 1971. *The Splendor of Iridescence.* New York: Dodd, Mead & Company.

Turpin, F. T. 2000. *Insect Appreciation,* 2nd edition. Dubuque, IA: Kendall/Hunt Publishing Company.

Waterman, C. F. 1981. *A History of Angling.* Tulsa, OK: Winchester Press.

II. THE SILK WE WEAR

Borg, F., and L. Pigorini. 1938. *Die Seidenspinner, ihre Zoologie, Biologie und Sucht.* [*The Silkworms, Their Zoology, Biology, and Rearing.*] Berlin: Verlag von Julius Springer.

Butenandt, A., R. Beckmann, and E. Hecker. 1959. Über den Sexual-Lockstoff des Seidenspinners *Bombyx mori:* Reindarstellung und Konstitution. [On the sexual attractant of the silkworm *Bombyx mori:* Purification and structure.] *Zeitschrift für Naturforschung* 14:283–284.

Dubos, R. J. 1950. *Louis Pasteur, Free Lance of Science.* Boston: Little, Brown and Company.

Emerson, A. I., and C. M. Weed. 1936. *Our Trees: How to Know Them.* Philadelphia: J. B. Lippincott.

Evans, R. 2005. Trump and circumstance. *Weddings in Style,* Spring, 262–269.

Fabre, J.-H. 1874. *The Great Peacock Moth.* Reprinted in *The Insect World of J. Henri Fabre,* ed. E. W. Teale, pp. 83–98. New York: Fawcett Publications, 1956.

Frank, K. D. 1986. History of the ailanthus silk moth (Lepidoptera: Saturniidae) in Philadelphia: A case study in urban ecology. *Entomological News* 97:41–51.

Kafatos, F. C., and C. M. Williams. 1964. Enzymatic mechanism for the escape of certain moths from their cocoons. *Science* 146:538–540.

Kelly, H. A. 1903. *The Culture of the Mulberry Silkworm.* USDA Division of Entomology Bulletin 39, new series.

Lutz, F. E. 1918. *Field Book of Insects.* New York: G. P. Putnam's Sons. (Reprinted 1935.)

McCook, H. C. 1886. *Tenants of an Old Farm.* New York: Fords, Howard & Hulbert.

National Academy of Sciences. 2003. Insect pheromones. In *Beyond Discovery: The Path from Research to Human Benefit.* www.beyonddiscovery.org.

Nicolson, J. U., trans. 1934. *Canterbury Tales.* New York: Garden City Publishing.

Nolan, E. J. 1892. The introduction of the ailanthus silk worm moth. *Entomological News* 3:193–195.

Oldroyd, H. 1964. *The Natural History of Flies.* New York: W. W. Norton.

Peigler, R. S. 1993. Wild silks of the world. *American Entomologist* 39:151–161.

Ross, G. N. 1986. The bug in the rug. *Natural History* 95:66–73.

Schoonhoven, L. M., T. Jermy, and J. J. A. van Loon. 1998. *Insect-Plant Biology.* London: Chapman and Hall.

Scott, P. 1993. *The Book of Silk.* London: Thames and Hudson.

Senechal, M. 2004. *Northampton's Century of Silk.* Northampton, MA: 350th Anniversary Committee of the City of Northampton.

Strayer, J. R., ed. 1983. *Dictionary of the Middle Ages.* New York: Charles Scribner's Sons.

Tuskes, P. M., J. P. Tuttle, and M. M. Collins. 1996. *The Wild Silk Moths of North America.* Ithaca, NY: Cornell University Press.

Vincent, J. M. 1935. *Costume and Conduct.* Baltimore: Johns Hopkins Press.

Waldbauer, G. P. 1982. The allocation of silk in the compact and baggy cocoons of *Hyalophora cecropia. Entomologia Experimentalis et Applicata* 31:191–196.

Waldbauer, G. P., and J. G. Sternburg. 1982. Cocoons of *Callosamia promethea* (Saturniidae): Adaptive significance of differences in mode of attachment to the host tree. *Journal of the Lepidopterists' Society* 36:192–199.

———. 1982. Long mating flights by male *Hyalophora cecropia* (L.) (Saturniidae). *Journal of the Lepidopterists' Society* 36:154–155.

Wigglesworth, V. B. 1972. *The Principles of Insect Physiology,* 7th edition. London: Chapman and Hall.

III. DYEING THE CLOTH

Brand, D. D. 1966. Cochineal: Aboriginal dyestuff from Nueva España. *Acta y Memorias de XXXVI Congreso Internacional de Americanistas, España 1964* 2:77–91.

Comstock, J. H. 1950. *An Introduction to Entomology,* 9th edition, revised. Ithaca, NY: Comstock Publishing Company.

Cowan, F. 1865. *Curious Facts in the History of Insects.* Philadelphia: J. B. Lippincott.

DeBach, P. 1964. *Biological Control of Insect Pests and Weeds.* New York: Reinhold Publishing.

Donkin, R. A. 1977. Spanish red: An ethnographical study of cochineal and the Opuntia cactus. *Transactions of the American Philosophical Society* 67:1–84.

Fagan, M. M. 1918. The uses of insect galls. *The American Naturalist* 52:155–176.

Hogue, C. L. 1993. *Latin American Insects and Entomology.* Berkeley and Los Angeles: University of California Press.

Jones, C. L. 1966. *Guatemala Past and Present.* New York: Russell and Russell.

Kosztarab, M. 1987. Everything unique or unusual about scale insects (Homoptera: Coccoidae). *Bulletin of the Entomological Society of America* 33:215–220.

Lauro, G. J. 1991. A primer on natural colors. *Cereal Foods World* 36:949–953.

Phipson, T. L. 1864. *The Utilization of Minute Life.* London: Goombridge and Sons.

Ross, G. N. 1986. The bug in the rug. *Natural History* 95:66–73.

IV. BAUBLES, BRACELETS, AND ANKLETS

Akre, R. D., A. Greene, J. F. MacDonald, P. J. Landolt, and H. G. Davis. 1980. *Yellowjackets of America North of Mexico.* USDA Agricultural Handbook, no. 552. Washington, DC: U.S. Government Printing Office.

Bates, C. D. 1992. Sierra Miwok shamans, 1900–1990. In *California Indian Shamanism,* ed. L. J. Bean, pp. 97–115. Menlo Park, CA: Ballena Press.

Beckmann, P. 2003. *Living Jewels.* London: Prestel Publishing.

Berlin, B., and G. T. Prance. 1978. Insect galls and human ornamentation: The ethnobotanical significance of a new species of *Licania* from Amazonas, Peru. *Biotropica* 10:81–86.

Cowan, F. 1865. *Curious Facts in the History of Insects.* Philadelphia: J. B. Lippincott.

Frisch, K. von. 1974. *Animal Architecture.* New York: Harcourt Brace Jovanovich.

Geijskes, D. C. 1975. The dragonfly wing used as a nose plug adornment. *Odonatologica* 4:29–30.

Howard, L. O. 1900. Two interesting uses of insects by natives in Natal. *Scientific American* 83:267.

Imms, A. D. 1951. *A General Textbook of Entomology.* London: Methuen.

Kirby, W., and W. Spence. 1846. *An Introduction to Entomology,* 6th edition. Philadelphia: Lea and Blanchard. (Originally published 1815.)

Linsenmaier, W. 1972. *Insects of the World.* Translated by L. E. Chadwick. New York: McGraw-Hill.

McCook, H. D. 1886. *Tenants of an Old Farm.* New York: Fords, Howard & Hulbert.

McMaster, G., and C. E. Trafzer, eds. 2004. *Native Universe: Voices of Indian America.* Washington, DC: National Geographic Society.

Parkman, E. B. 1992. Dancing on the brink of the world: Deprivation and the ghost dance religion. In *California Indian Shamanism,* ed. L. J. Bean, pp. 163–183. Menlo Park, CA: Ballena Press.

Peigler, R. S. 1994. *Non-sericultural Uses of Moth Cocoons in Diverse Cultures.* Proceedings of the Denver Museum of Natural History, ser. 3, no. 5.

Schultze, A. 1913. *Die wichtigsten Seidenspinner Afrikas mit besonderer Berücksichtigung der Gesellschaftersspinner.* [*The Most Important Silkworms of Africa with Particular Attention to the Social Silkworm.*] London: African Silk Corp. Ltd.

Schwarz, H. F. 1948. *Stingless Bees (Meliponidae) of the Western Hemisphere.* Bulletin of the American Museum of Natural History 90.

Turpin, F. T. 2000. *Insect Appreciation,* 2nd edition. Dubuque, IA: Kendall/Hunt Publishing Company.

Wilkinson, R. W. 1969. Colloquia entomologica II: A remarkable sale of Victorian entomological jewelry. *The Michigan Entomologist* 2:77–81.

V. CANDLES, SHELLAC, AND SEALING WAX

Berenbaum, M. R. 1995. *Bugs in the System.* Reading, MA: Addison-Wesley.

Bishop, H. 2005. *Robbing the Bees.* New York: Free Press.

Bishopp, F. C. 1952. Insect friends of man. In *Yearbook of Agriculture, 1952,* pp. 79–87. Washington, DC: U.S. Government Printing Office.

Comstock, J. H. 1950. *An Introduction to Entomology,* 9th edition, revised. Ithaca, NY: Comstock Publishing Company.

Cowan, F. 1865. *Curious Facts in the History of Insects.* Philadelphia: J. B. Lippincott.

Crandall, E. B. 1924. *Shellac, a Story of Yesterday, Today and Tomorrow.* Chicago: James B. Day & Co.

Essig, E. O. 1931. *A History of Entomology.* New York: Macmillan.

Friedmann, H. 1955. *The Honey-Guides.* U.S. National Museum, bulletin 208.

Jenkins, K. D. 1970. The fat-yielding coccid, *Llaveia,* a monophlebine of the Margarodidae. *Pan-Pacific Entomologist* 46:79–81.

Kosztarab, M. 1987. Everything unique or unusual about scale insects (Homoptera: Coccoidea). *Bulletin of the Entomological Society of America* 33:215–220.

Langstroth, L. L. 1853. *On the Hive and the Honey-Bee.* Medina, OH: A. I. Root. (Reprinted 1914.)

Lindauer, M. 1967. *Communication among Social Bees.* New York: Athenium.

Metcalf, R. L., and R. A. Metcalf. 1993. *Destructive and Useful Insects,* 5th edition. New York: McGraw Hill.

Michener, C. D. 1974. *The Social Behavior of the Bees.* Cambridge, MA: Harvard University Press.

Miller, D. R., and M. Kosztarab. 1979. Recent advances in the study of scale insects. *Annual Review of Entomology* 24:1–27.

Morse, R. A. 1975. *Bees and Beekeeping.* Ithaca, NY: Cornell University Press.

Newberry, P. E. 1976. *Ancient Egyptian Scarabs.* Chicago: Ares Publishers. (Reprint of the 1905 London edition.)

Ono, M., T. Igarashi, E. Ohno, and M. Sasaki. 1995. Unusual thermal defense by a honeybee against mass attacks by hornets. *Science* 377:334–336.

Peters, T. M. 1988. *Insects and Human Society.* New York: Van Nostrand and Reinhold.

Schwarz, H. F. 1948. *Stingless Bees (Meliponidae) of the Western Hemisphere.* Bulletin of the American Museum of Natural History 90.

Weis, H. B. 1927. The scarabaeus of the ancient Egyptians. *The American Naturalist* 61:353–369.

Wigglesworth, V. B. 1945. Transpiration through the cuticle of insects. *Journal of Experimental Biology* 21:97–114.

VI. PAPER AND INK

Borror, D. J., D. M. De Long, and C. A. Triplehorn. 1981. *An Introduction to the Study of Insects.* Philadelphia: Saunders College Publishing.

Claiborne, R. 1974. *The Birth of Writing.* Alexandria, VA: Time-Life Books.

Cowan, F. 1865. *Curious Facts in the History of Insects.* Philadelphia: J. B. Lippincott.

Ebert, J. 2005. Tongue tied. *Nature* 438:148–149.

Fagan, M. M. 1918. The uses of insect galls. *The American Naturalist* 52:155–176.

Felt, E. P. 1965. *Plant Galls and Gall Makers.* New York: Hafner Publishing Company. (Facsimile of the 1940 edition.)

Gallencamp, C. 1959. *Maya.* New York: Pyramid Publications.

Gullan, P.J., and P.S. Cranston. 1994. *The Insects: An Outline of Entomology.* London: Chapman and Hall.

Hocking, B. 1968. *Six-Legged Science.* Cambridge, MA: Schenkman Publishing.

Hogue, C. L. 1987. Cultural entomology. *Annual Review of Entomology* 32:181–199.

Kevan, P. G., and R. A. Bye. 1991. The natural history, sociobiology, and ethnobiology of *Eucheira socialis* Westwood (Lepidoptera: Pieridae), a unique and little-known butterfly from Mexico. *The Entomologist* 110:146–165.

Kinsey, A. C. 1929. *The Gall Wasp Genus Cynips.* Indiana University Studies, vol. 16. Bloomington: Indiana University Press.

Lawler, A. 2004. The slow deaths of writing. *Science* 305:30–33.

Peigler, R. S. 1993. Wild silks of the world. *American Entomologist* 39:151–161.

Spradbery, J. P. 1973. *Wasps.* Seattle: University of Washington Press.

Tsai, J. H. 1982. Entomology in the People's Republic of China. *Journal of the New York Entomological Society* 90:186–212.

Weis, A. E., and M. R. Berenbaum. 1989. Herbivorous insects and green plants. In *Plant-Animal Interactions,* ed. W. G. Abrahamson, pp. 123–162. New York: McGraw-Hill.

Wilson, E. O. 2006. The civilized insect. *National Geographic* 210:136–149.

VII. BUTTERFLIES IN YOUR TUMMY

Aldrich, J. M. 1912. The biology of some western species of the dipterous genus *Ephydra. Journal of the New York Entomological Society* 20:77–98.

———. 1921. *Coloradia pandora* Blake, a moth of which the caterpillar is used as a food by the Mono Lake Indians. *Annals of the Entomological Society of America* 14:36–38.

Bequaert, J. 1921. Insects as food. *Natural History: The Journal of the American Museum of Natural History* 21:191–200.

Blake, E. A., and M. R. Wagner. 1987. Collection and consumption of pandora moth, *Coloradia pandora* (Lepidoptera: Saturniidea), larvae by Owens Valley and Mono Lake Paiutes. *Bulletin of the Entomological Society of America* 33:23–27.

Bodenheimer, F. S. 1951. *Insects as Human Food.* The Hague: W. Junk.

Bristowe, W. S. 1932. Insects and other invertebrates for human consumption in Siam. *Transactions of the Entomological Society of London* 80:387–404.

Cherry, R. H. 1991. Use of insects by Australian Aborigines. *American Entomologist* 37:9–13.

China, W. E. 1931. An interesting relationship between a crayfish and a water bug. *Natural History Magazine* 3:57–62.

DeFoliart, G. R. 1989. The human use of insects as food and as animal feed. *Bulletin of the Entomological Society of America* 35:22–35.

———. 1992. Insects as human food. *Crop Protection* 11:395–399.

———. 1999. Insects as food: Why the Western attitude is important. *Annual Review of Entomology* 44:21–50.

Goodall, J. 1963. Feeding behaviour of wild chimpanzees. *Symposia of the Zoological Society of London* 10:39–47.

Holt, V. M. 1885. *Why Not Eat Insects?* London: British Museum (Natural History). (Reprinted 1988.)

Noyes, H. 1937. *Man and the Termite.* London: Peter Davies.

Pemberton, R. W. 1988. The use of the Thai giant waterbug, *Lethocerus indicus* (Hemiptera: Belastomatidae), as human food in California. *Pan-Pacific Entomologist* 64:81–82.

Pemberton, R. W., and T. Yamasaki. 1995. Insects: Old food in new Japan. *American Entomologist* 41:227–229.

Remington, C. L. 1946. Insects as food in Japan. *Entomological News* 57:119–121.

Riley, C. V. 1876. *Noxious, Beneficial, and Other Insects of the State of Missouri.* Eighth Annual Report to the Missouri State Board of Agriculture. Jefferson City, MO: Regan and Carter.

Taylor, R. L. 1975. *Butterflies in My Stomach.* Santa Barbara, CA: Woodbridge Press.

Tindale, N. B. 1966. Insects as food for the Australian Aborigines. *Australian Natural History* 15:179–183.

Vane-Wright, R. I. 1991. Why not eat insects? *Bulletin of Entomological Research* 81:1–4.

Van Tyne, J. 1951. A cardinal's, *Richmondena cardinalis,* choice of food for adult and for young. *Auk* 68:110.

VIII. SATISFYING THE SWEET TOOTH

Anderson, C., and F. L. W. Ratnieks. 1999. Worker allocation in insect societies: Coordination of nectar foragers and nectar receivers in honey bee (*Apis mellifera*) colonies. *Behavioral Ecology and Sociobiology* 46:73–81.

Barber, [no first name given]. 1905. [No title.] *Entomological Society of Washington* 7:25.

Belt, T. 1888. *The Naturalist in Nicaragua.* London: Edward Bumpus.

Bishop, H. 2005. *Robbing the Bees.* New York: Free Press.

Bodenheimer, F. S. 1951. *Insects as Human Food.* The Hague: W. Junk.

Chakrabarti, K. 1987. Sundabarans honey and the mangrove swamps. *Journal of the Bombay Natural History Society* 84:133–137.

Crane, E. 1980. *A Book of Honey.* Oxford: Oxford University Press.

———. 1999. *The World History of Beekeeping and Honey Hunting.* New York: Routledge.

DeMera, J. H., and E. R. Angert. 2004. Comparison of the antimicrobial activity of honey produced by *Tetragonisca angustula* (Meliponinae) and *Apis mellifera* from different phytogeographic regions of Costa Rica. *Apidologie* 35:411–417.

Dornhaus, A., and L. Chittka. 2004. Why do honey bees dance? *Behavioral Ecology and Sociobiology* 55:395–401.

Evans, H. E., and M. J. W. Eberhard. 1970. *The Wasps.* Ann Arbor: University of Michigan Press.

Frisch, K. von. 1953. *The Dancing Bees,* 5th revised edition. Translated by D. Ilse. New York: Harcourt, Brace, and World.

———. 1967. *The Dance Language and Orientation of the Bees.* Translated by L. E. Chadwick. Cambridge, MA: Harvard University Press.

———. 1971. *Bees,* revised edition. Translated by L. E. Chadwick. Ithaca, NY: Cornell University Press.

Gary, N. E. 1975. Activities and behavior of honey bees. In *The Hive and the Honey Bee,* ed. Dadant & Sons, pp. 185–264. Hamilton, IL: Dadant & Sons.

Kennedy, J. S., and T. E. Mittler. 1953. A method for obtaining phloem sap via the mouth-parts of aphids. *Nature* 171:528.

Michener, C. D. 1974. *The Social Behavior of the Bees.* Cambridge, MA: Harvard University Press.

Morse, R. A. 1980. *Making Mead.* Ithaca, NY: Wicwas Press.

Newberry, P. E. 1905. *Ancient Egyptian Scarabs.* Chicago: Ares Publishers. (Reprint of the 1905 London edition.)

Nicolson, J. U., trans. 1934. *Canterbury Tales.* New York: Garden City Publishing.

Oldroyd, B. P., and S. Wongsiri. 2006. *Asian Honey Bees.* Cambridge, MA: Harvard University Press.

Ransome, H. M. 1937. *The Sacred Bee.* Boston: Houghton Mifflin.

Saunders, W. 1875. The Mexican honey ant. *Canadian Entomologist* 7:12–14.

Schwarz, H. F. 1948. *Stingless Bees (Meliponidae) of the Western Hemisphere.* Bulletin of the American Museum of Natural History 90.

Snodgrass, R. E. 1956. *Anatomy of the Honey Bee.* Ithaca, NY: Cornell University Press.
Spencer, B. 1928. *Wanderings in Wild Australia,* vols. 1 and 2. London: Macmillan.
Spradbery, J. P. 1973. *Wasps.* Seattle: University of Washington Press.
Stumper R. 1961. Radiobiologische Untersuchungen über den sozialen Nahrungshaushalt der Honigameise *Proformica nasuta* (Nyl). [Radiobiologic studies of the social nutritional economy of the honey ant *Proformica nasuta* (Nyl).] *Naturwissenschaften* 48:735–736.
Wheeler, W. M. 1908. Honey ants, with a revision of the American *Myrmecocysti. Bulletin of the American Museum of Natural History* 24:345–397.
Wilson, E. O. 1971. *The Insect Societies.* Cambridge, MA: Harvard University Press.

IX. CURES AND NOSTRUMS

Baer, W. S. 1931. The treatment of chronic osteomyelitis with the maggot (larva of the blow fly). *Journal of Bone and Joint Surgery* 13:438–475.
Beebe, W. 1921. *Edge of the Jungle.* New York: Henry Holt and Company.
Cowan, F. 1865. *Curious Facts in the History of Insects.* Philadelphia: J. B. Lippincott.
Crane, E. 1980. *A Book of Honey.* Oxford: Oxford University Press.
Dawood, N. J., trans. 2003. *The Koran*. London: Penguin Books.
Gudger, E. W. 1925. Stitching wounds with the mandibles of ants and beetles. *Journal of the American Medical Association* 84:1861–1864.
Hogue, C. L. 1987. Cultural entomology. *Annual Review of Entomology* 32:181–199.
Kramer, S. N. 1954. First pharmacopeia in man's recorded history. *American Journal of Pharmacy* 126:76–84.
Majno, G. 1975. *The Healing Hand.* Cambridge, MA: Harvard University Press.
Maynard, B. 2006. Take two *what* and call you in the morning? *National Wildlife,* February/March, 16–17.
Metcalf, R. L., and R. A. Metcalf. 1993. *Destructive and Useful Insects,* 5th edition. New York: McGraw-Hill.
Pliny the Elder. 1856. *The Natural History of Pliny.* Ed. and trans. J. Bostock and H. T. Riley. London: Henry G. Bohn.
Ransome, H. M. 1937. *The Sacred Bee.* Boston: Houghton Mifflin.
Robinson, W. 1935. Allantoin, a constituent of maggot excretions, stimulates healing of chronic discharging wounds. *Journal of Parasitology* 21:354–358.
Sherman, R. A. 2000. Maggot therapy—the last five years. *Bulletin of the European Tissue Repair Society* 7:97–98.

Sherman, R.A., M.J.R. Hall, and S. Thomas. 2000. Medicinal maggots: An ancient remedy for some contemporary afflictions. *Annual Review of Entomology* 45:55–81.

Sherman, R.A., and E.A. Pechter. 1988. Maggot therapy: A review of the therapeutic applications of fly larvae in human medicine, especially for treating osteomyelitis. *Medical and Veterinary Entomology* 2:225–230.

Subrahmanyan, M. 1998. A prospective randomized clinical and histological study of superficial burn wound healing with honey and silver sulfadiazine. *Burns* 24:157–161.

Traynor, J. 2002. *Honey, the Gourmet Medicine.* Bakersfield, CA: Kovak Books.

Willson, R.B., and E. Crane. 1975. Uses and products of honey. In *Honey: A Comprehensive Survey,* ed. E. Crane, pp. 378–391. New York: Crane, Russak and Company.

Wood, J.G. 1883. *Insects at Home.* New York: John B. Alden.

X. INSECT PETS AND PERFORMERS

Alcock, J. 1993. *Animal Behavior,* 5th edition. Sunderland, MA: Sinauer Associates.

Barth, R.H., Jr. 1968. The mating behavior of *Gromphadorhina portentosa* (Schaum) (Blattaria, Blaberoidea, Blaberidae, Oxyhaloinae): An anomalous pattern for a cockroach. *Psyche* 75:124–131.

Borror, D.J., D.M. DeLong, and C.A. Triplehorn. 1981. *An Introduction to the Study of Insects.* Philadelphia: Saunders.

Comstock, J.H. 1950. *An Introduction to Entomology,* 9th edition, revised. Ithaca, NY: Comstock Publishing Company.

Cowan, F. 1865. *Curious Facts in the History of Insects.* Philadelphia: J.B. Lippincott.

Dall, W.H. 1877. Educated fleas. *American Naturalist* 11:7–11.

Dethier, V.G. 1992. *Crickets and Katydids, Concerts and Solos.* Cambridge, MA: Harvard University Press.

Goff, M.L. 2000. *A Fly for the Prosecution.* Cambridge, MA: Harvard University Press.

Hall, E.R., and W.C. Russell. 1933. Dermestid beetles as an aid in cleaning bones. *Journal of Mammalogy* 14:372–374.

Hearn, L. 1898. *Exotics and Retrospectives.* Boston: Little, Brown.

Hsu, Y.C. 1928. Crickets in China. *Peking Society of Natural History Bulletin* 3:5–41.

Kevan, D.K.M., and C.C. Hsiung. 1976. Cricket-fighting in Hong Kong. *Bulletin of the Entomological Society of Canada* 8:11–12.

Laufer, B. 1927. *Insect-Musicians and Cricket Champions of China.* Leaflet 22. Chicago: Field Museum of Natural History.

Lord, W.D. 1990. Case histories of the use of insects in investigations. In *Entomology and Death: A Procedural Guide,* ed. E. P. Catts and N. H. Haskell, pp. 9–37. Clemson, SC: Joyce's Print Shop.

Matthews, R. W., and J. R. Matthews. 1978. *Insect Behavior.* New York: John Wiley and Sons.

Pemberton, R. W. 1994. Japanese singing insects. www.insects.org/ced3/japanese_sing.html.

Phillips, L. H., II, and M. Konishi. 1973. Control of aggression by singing in crickets. *Nature* 241:64–65.

Roth, L. M. 1970. Evolution and taxonomic significance of reproduction in Blattaria. *Annual Review of Entomology* 15:75–96.

Tweedie, M. 1969. *Pleasure from Insects.* New York: Taplinger Publishing Company.

Villiard, P. 1969. *Moths and How to Rear Them.* New York: Funk and Wagnalls.

———. 1973. *Insects as Pets.* New York: Doubleday.

Acknowledgments

Thanks to the many friends and colleagues who gave freely of their time, expertise, and advice to make this book considerably better than it would have been without their support. Among them are May Berenbaum, Sam Beshers, Douglas Brewer, Sydney Cameron, Fred Gottheil, Larry Hanks, M. Andrew Heckman, Yoko Muroga, James Nardi, Tom Newman, Gene Robinson, Sheila Ryan, Kazuko Sasamori, David Secrest, Art Siedler, Susan Slottow, James Sternburg, Charles Whitfield, James Whitfield, and Masako Yamamoto. I am especially grateful to Phyllis Cooper, who read the entire manuscript and made innumerable helpful suggestions, and to my agent, Edward Knappman of New England Publishing Associates. And many thanks to Jenny Wapner, Laura Harger, and Madeleine Adams, whose suggestions and editing greatly improved this book.

Index

Page numbers in italics indicate illustrations.

Designer: Lia Tjandra
Text: 12/16 Vendetta
Display: Bodoni
Illustrator: James Nardi
Indexer: Kevin Millham
Compositor: Integrated Composition Systems
Printer and Binder: Sheridan Books, Inc.